A Colorado Kind of Christmas

Treasured Rocky Mountain Yuletide Traditions

Christmas is coming...

A Colorado Kind of Christmas

Treasured Rocky Mountain Yuletide Traditions

Collected and Edited by

LAURA McCLURE DIRKS

AND

SALLY HEWITT DANIEL

WESTCLIFFE PUBLISHERS, INC.
ENGLEWOOD, COLORADO

A portion of the proceeds from the mail order and phone sales of this book will benefit the Colorado Children's Chorale. To order additional copies, write or call:

A Colorado Kind of Christmas
Westcliffe Publishers, Inc.
P.O. Box 1261, Dept. CC
Englewood, Colorado 80150-1261

303-935-0900 in Colorado or 1-800-523-3692 from out of state.
(Please mention Colorado Children's Chorale when ordering.)

The Colorado Children's Chorale also offers *A Colorado Kind of Christmas* tape and CD. To place your order, please use the reply cards located in the back of the book.

International Standard Book Number: 1-56579-048-0
Library of Congress Catalogue Number: 93-060291

Published by Westcliffe Publishers, Englewood, Colorado
John Fielder, Publisher
Suzanne Venino, Managing Editor
Leslie L. Gerarden, Creative Director

Design by Rob Johnson, Wilson-Johnson Creative, Denver, Colorado
Nature photography by John Fielder
Christmas photography by Brian Litz (unless otherwise noted)
Food styling by Epicurean Catering, Denver, Colorado
Bonnie Beach, Copy Editor/Proofreader
Printed in Singapore by Tien Wah Press (Pte.), Ltd.

Reprinted with permission:
Music & lyrics for "Christmas in Colorado" by Samuel B. Lancaster
Descant for "Silent Night" by Duain Wolfe

Scripture verses are excerpted from the Holy Bible, King James Version

A Colorado Kind of Christmas is a trademark of Dirks & Daniel Companies.

Dedicated to:

The Candy House Kids

Katy

William

Anne

Katherine

Michael

J.T.

Ashley

Katy

Katie

Beth

Hewitt

and Aunt Fran

Welcome Home
to A Colorado Kind of Christmas

In 1989, we had both just turned forty, our children were growing up, and we had experienced the deaths of close, beloved family members. In short, we were each having a mid-life crisis! During the busiest time of the Christmas season, we found ourselves attending a very special Christmas program performed by the Colorado Children's Chorale. As sometimes happens, this performance was significant because it triggered thoughts about how we were living our lives and the legacies we were leaving our children.

Living in Colorado, as wonderful as it is, has separated both of us from relatives and loved ones. We come from different regions of the country—Laura from the Midwest, and Sally from the South. After having lived here for more than 20 years, we have adapted our own childhood Christmas traditions to the Colorado lifestyle. We came to realize that these holiday celebrations would form the basis for our children's traditions for the rest of their lives.

Christmas in Colorado means snow, skiing, sleigh rides, caroling, candlelit church services, or a trek into the forest to find just the right Christmas tree. How could we collectively save these experiences for ourselves, our children, and others? The idea for *A Colorado Kind of Christmas* was born from those discussions and from a determination to discover just what a "real" Colorado Christmas is.

As we talked about Christmas in Colorado and how it differed from the family traditions we grew up with, we realized that there were others in the same situation. Just like the pioneers of a century ago, many present-day Coloradans have moved here from other places, leaving behind family and friends in distant states. They, too, have tailored their holiday traditions to their new home. We wanted to portray our adopted state, its people, and their very special Christmas celebrations.

Our Christmas traditions are a blend of the past and the present, the result of our upbringings as well as the influences of living amid the snow-covered mountains of Colorado—the perfect holiday setting. In considering this, we began to see that traditions are formed through the repetition of family customs, and we wanted to examine our own Christmas traditions, as well as those of fellow Coloradans. We believe it is important to honor these traditions and pass them on—along with the stories of their origins—to our children.

Because a book like this needs to be based on fact, we began to research. We thought we knew quite a bit about Christmas in Colorado—but we didn't. After contacting every historical museum, chamber of commerce, resort association, and arts and humanities council that we could find, we then asked thousands of individuals to describe what "a Colorado kind of Christmas" meant to them. Their responses have been compiled in this collection, and we invite you to enjoy it and recall your own treasured memories and traditions as you celebrate the Christmas season.

Laura & Sally

P.S. If you would like to share memories, traditions or recipes with us, please write to "The Christmas Ladies" in care of Westcliffe Publishers.

Contents

Snow patterns of spring, Crested Butte

Fresh snow, Rabbit Ears Pass

Christmas in Colorado

Lyrics and music by Samuel B. Lancaster

Climb up to the top of Look-out Moun-tain and look out to the east at the

lights of the cit-ies, twinkling like stars in a sky of fenced and fur-rowed fields. It's

Christ-mas in Co-lo-ra-do. Then turn the oth-er way and look on mountains

stretch-ing to the west. See the peaks of the Rockies, gi-ant snow stars top-ping

waves of liv-ing Christ-mas trees. It's Christ-mas in Co-lo-ra-do.

Christ-mas is the time when we long to have a star, our own star that will lead us on our

Sunset, Collegiate Peaks Wilderness

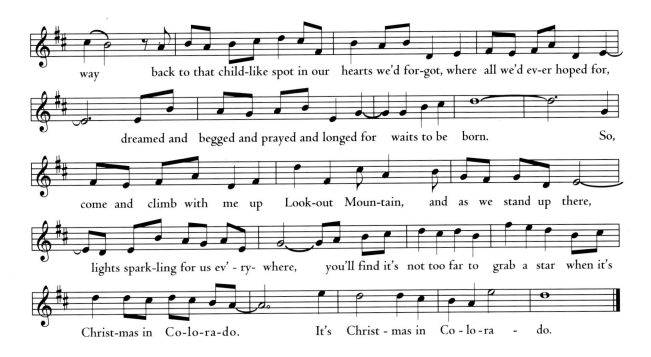

way back to that child-like spot in our hearts we'd for-got, where all we'd ev-er hoped for,

dreamed and begged and prayed and longed for waits to be born. So,

come and climb with me up Look-out Moun-tain, and as we stand up there,

lights spark-ling for us ev' - ry- where, you'll find it's not too far to grab a star when it's

Christ-mas in Co-lo-ra-do. It's Christ - mas in Co - lo - ra - do.

Editor's Note: "Christmas in Colorado," by Samuel B. Lancaster, was a gift to the
Colorado Children's Chorale.

Home Celebrations

Preparing for family and friends to spend Christmas in
Colorado is a labor of love. Whether we celebrate at home or
while vacationing in the state, the anticipation of the season
heightens the excitement. Why? Because Christmas is not just a time
of year, but a place in our hearts, a place we create through memories.
These cherished memories are brought out each year for reminiscing and
celebrating anew. ❆ Home. The sights and smells of Christmases past
and those yet to come help us realize the value of our own special
traditions. Homes festooned with decorations remind us that Christmas
is near. This is the time of year when we bring out the holly and the
mistletoe. In Colorado we also decorate our very own Colorado blue
spruce trees, both indoors and out. The smell of fresh evergreen
permeates the house, a sure sign that Christmas is coming. ❆
Cookies bake in the oven, filling the house with the warmth of
the season. The laughter of little children, trying to be extra
good in case Santa is watching, adds to the holiday
atmosphere. Ornaments—many handmade, others
passed down through generations—are hung with
care on the tree. The traditions of the season
remind us that home is where we
make it and that Christmas is
a time of love.

*** ❄ ❄ ❄ ***

The Night
Before Christmas
by Clement C. Moore

'Twas the night

before Christmas,

when all through

the house

Not a creature

was stirring, not

even a mouse;

The stockings were

hung by the

chimney with care,

A traditional celebration for Coloradans, as well as many others, is gathering around the fireplace to read The Night Before Christmas.

One of the most touching readings of this story takes place every year at the historic Hamill House in Georgetown.

During the weeks before Christmas, the local historical society celebrates with several evenings of dining and festivities. After dinner and caroling, children read the story aloud as part of the tree-lighting ceremony.

Written in 1822 by Clement C. Moore and originally titled The Visit of St. Nicholas, *the beloved story of Santa's magical visit is printed here in its entirety for your own holiday celebrations.*

*V*ictorian Christmas traditions are common throughout the state of Colorado. Many of these customs were imported directly from England, brought here by gold and silver barons during the mining booms of the late nineteenth and early twentieth centuries.

The legacy of our Victorian past, blended with the natural ruggedness of Colorado, brings a rustic elegance to the homes, decorations, and celebrations of Colorado Christmases. Most people envision the ideal Colorado Christmas as a cozy cabin nestled high in the mountains, surrounded by high peaks blanketed in snow. Inside, a blazing fire warms family and friends gathered round to roast chestnuts, sing carols, and toast the season with a traditional wassail. In this perfect setting, there are presents for everyone, our favorite foods…and someone else to do the dishes!

While reality may not necessarily match this picture, we nevertheless celebrate the holidays with family and friends and much-loved customs. Our home may not be the cozy cabin and there may not always be an abundance of presents, but we do have the mountains, the snow…and the dream of the perfect Christmas in Colorado.

*O*ur family tradition is to go to church on Christmas Eve, then have chicken soup for dinner and read The Night Before Christmas *by the fire. Our edition was my Mom's and is from 1949.*

— B.O'G., Littleton

❄ ❄ ❄

In hopes that

Saint Nicholas soon

would be there;

The children were

nestled all snug

in their beds,

While visions of

sugar-plums danced

through their heads;

One of the ways that we celebrate at home is to cut and decorate the tree. This is often one of the first things families do together at Christmas. Making special ornaments and trimming the tree heightens the anticipation of the season, and what better way to do this than by joining together for a family meal. This menu is simple and it makes for a festive beginning to the holidays.

❉ ❉ ❉

And mamma in her

kerchief, and I in

my cap, Had just

settled our brains

for a long

winter's nap,

When out on the

lawn there arose

such a clatter,

I sprang from my

bed to see what

was the matter.

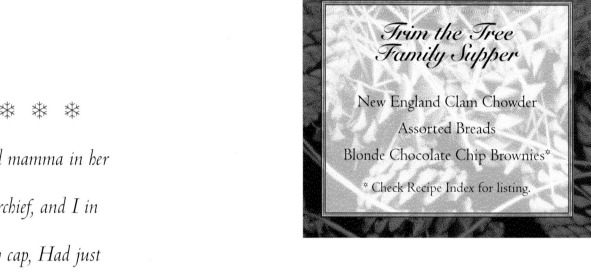

Trim the Tree
Family Supper

New England Clam Chowder

Assorted Breads

Blonde Chocolate Chip Brownies*

* Check Recipe Index for listing.

New England Clam Chowder

I usually serve this on Christmas Eve for the family and neighbors. It's easy and homey and cozy by the fire. I serve it with cranberry muffins, banana bread, fresh bread sticks, and croissants in baskets lined with Christmas napkins.

4 tablespoons butter	1 cup cream
½ cup onion, minced	4½ cups milk
½ cup green pepper, minced	1 teaspoon worcestershire sauce
½ cup celery, diced	1 teaspoon Accent
1 cup potato, diced	1 teaspoon salt
6 tablespoons flour	¼ teaspoon thyme
30 ounces of canned clams	6 drops Tabasco

In a heavy pan or Dutch oven, melt butter and saute onion, celery, and green pepper until tender—about eight minutes. Add the flour to the pan and blend until smooth. Drain the clams and add the broth to the pan. Stir in cream, milk, potatoes, and the remaining ingredients. Over medium heat, bring the soup to a boil, then immediately reduce heat and simmer 40 minutes, or until potatoes are tender. Add the clams and let soup cool for 5 minutes. Preparation time is 1½ hours, but the chowder can also be made ahead and frozen. Serves 8.

— Heidi Keogh

Thanksgiving marks the beginning of the Christmas season. It is a time to remember all that we have to be thankful for and a time to begin planning for the coming holidays. Entertaining family and friends is an integral part of the season, and getting ready is half the fun. Coloradans from all over the state wrote to tell us how they prepare for Christmas.

Christmas is coming...

We decorate the tree and set up the trains and village under it the day after Thanksgiving!

— Anonymous, Grand Junction

We hang our stockings on December 5 to celebrate the feast of Saint Nicholas. They are filled on the morning of December 6, and this begins our Christmas holidays.

— S.N., Littleton

Our family always decorates our tree two days after "Turkeyday." During the year we search for special ornaments to collect and place on the tree. Mom writes our names and the year on each ornament so we can remember that special year.

— K.D., Englewood

We decorate the house with lights.

— The M.F. Family, Steamboat Springs

In 1973, our young son, Chad, wrote a letter to Santa asking for a "golden trumpet." We lived in Steamboat Springs where on Christmas Eve, Santa arrived on a flatbed truck complete with Christmas music and a fully decorated and lighted tree. Santa then went door to door passing out Christmas stockings and candy.

That Christmas Eve the snow was so high that it came up to the window panes. The opportunity for our son to receive his special gift directly from Santa prompted my husband to sneak out the back door with the trumpet and hide in the snow banks until Santa was near. Our hearts were filled with joy as we watched Santa present the special gift.

— The Williams Family, Steamboat Springs

We have Advent calendars for the kids.

— S.C., Evergreen

We decorate with special ornaments every year. Often they are homemade and when the children are grown they will get them. Throughout the year I do my Christmas shopping at crafts fairs and vacation spots so that I have more free time during the holidays.

— D.L., Fort Collins

❄ ❄ ❄

Away to the window I flew like a flash, Tore open the shutters, and threw up the sash.

$\mathcal{M}$any personal accounts of how Coloradans celebrate their Christmases were shared with us. This story, taken from a diary, seemed to convey the special feelings and pride each family has in celebrating the season in their own way.

November 23

We had a really fun day decorating for Christmas. Denae, 4, wanted to wear her most recently acquired hand-me-down dress, a dark green calico trimmed with lace and velvet. First we walked to the mall to wave at Santa. Later, at home, we decorated a small tree with nativities cut from Christmas cards and glued in old jar lids. They were trimmed and hung with red ribbons.

We decorated our tree while "Come on Ring Those Bells" by Evie Carlson was playing. I had some blonde chocolate chip brownies ready to come out of the oven to eat when we finished decorating.

Denae taped Christmas cards on the door and put candles in an Advent wreath. She danced with Daddy in her beautiful dress to Christmas music, laughing and having a great time. We made a fun game of putting up the mistletoe, seeing who was going to get kissed. What a great time!

When David, 15 months, woke up from his nap, he noticed every new decoration. He filled our home and hearts with ooohhs and aaahhs as he pointed his chubby finger at each one.

— From the diary of Donna Burns, Littleton

The moon, on the

breast of the

new-fallen snow,

Gave a luster

of midday to

objects below;

Blonde Chocolate Chip Brownies

⅔ cup shortening	½ teaspoon salt
2¼ cups brown sugar	1 teaspoon vanilla
3 eggs	6 ounces chocolate chips
2¾ cups flour	1 cup nuts (optional)
2½ teaspoons baking powder	

Cream shortening and brown sugar, then mix in the eggs. Stir in the remaining ingredients. Pat brownie mix into a greased 8½ x 11-inch pan. Bake at 350 degrees for 20 to 25 minutes. DO NOT over bake. Cut into bars before cooling completely. Makes 3 dozen.

Majeski Family Christmas

While in college, we could not afford many Christmas decorations or gifts, so we baked fruitcake using the old family recipe to give to friends and relatives.

In order to save the eggs to make into ornaments, we didn't break them. We made small pin pricks and blew out the insides, then we painted the eggs with lacquer.

That first Christmas we had one string of lights and 24 eggs on the tree. Through the years we have accumulated more lights, and the tradition of decorating eggs has persisted.

Using a variety of techniques, we now have 12 dozen eggs, which are the only ornaments we use. They have become our most prized Christmas possessions, and unpacking them each year is a very special part of our holiday season.

— Sue and Ken Majeski,
Denver

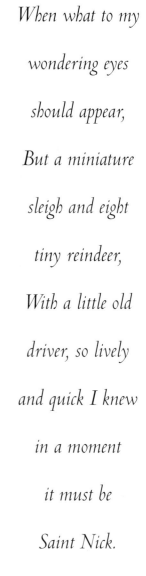

❄ ❄ ❄

When what to my

wondering eyes

should appear,

But a miniature

sleigh and eight

tiny reindeer,

With a little old

driver, so lively

and quick I knew

in a moment

it must be

Saint Nick.

aking Christmas cookies is a memorable part of the holiday season. The aroma wafting through the house beckons you to the kitchen to snitch a few fresh from the oven.

Because Christmas is such a busy time, a "cookie exchange" is an ideal way to have a variety of homemade cookies on hand during the holidays. The concept is simple: throw a party and have each guest bring several dozen homemade cookies of her favorite recipe; when the guests have traded cookies with each other, they all go home with as many as ten to twelve different kinds of cookies!

Cyndi Duncan and Georgie Patrick of Greeley have perfected the art of the cookie exchange, which they describe in their cookbook, Colorado Cookie Collection. *Here are some of their suggestions.*

HOW TO HOST A
Cookie Exchange

Planning:

With a friend, pick a date, time, and place. Then make a guest list. On your invitations indicate how many cookies guests should bring and instruct them to RSVP by sending their cookie recipe to the hostess.

Preparation:

Copy the recipes into a booklet for each guest to take home. Make name tags in several holiday patterns. Make two place cards for each cookie recipe, including the name of the cookie and the baker. Bake your own cookies.

On the day of the party, set up a refreshment area, including a tasting table, plates, napkins, and drinks—coffee, tea, or punch. Put one place card for each recipe next to a plate for each guest's sample cookies. In another room, prepare a cookie exchange buffet. It should include the second cookie place card and a box for each guest to use to collect the assorted cookies. If you have a large group, you may want to enlist two to four young helpers.

The Exchange:

Greet your guests at the door. Helpers take coats and hand out name tags and recipe booklets. Guests fill out address labels for invitations to next year's cookie exchange and are then directed to the refreshment area.

The helpers arrange six to twelve samples of each cookie on the tasting table. The remaining cookies are placed on the exchange buffet with the second identifying place card.

When all guests have arrived, the helpers select an assortment of cookies for each hostess and set them aside. The helpers stay at the exchange buffet to assist the guests. The hostess draws a name from the pre-addressed labels, and the group of guests whose name tags match the holiday pattern of the chosen name are invited to select cookies. Repeat this process until everyone has selected some cookies. Guests leave with a recipe booklet and a wide selection of cookies to enjoy throughout the Christmas season.

❄ ❄ ❄

More rapid than

eagles his coursers

they came, And he

whistled and

shouted and called

them by name:

Cookie Exchange Favorites

Bizcochitos*
Cranberry Date Bars*
Eggnog Cookies*
Fudge Bill Likes!*
Gingerbread Boys*
Grandma Chrismer's Christmas Sugar Cookies
Kris Kringles*
Nana's Cookies*
Overnight Meringue Cookies*
White Fruit Cake*

*Check Recipe Index for these listings.

Grandma Chrismer's Christmas Sugar Cookies

My mother's recipe has been a favorite tradition in our family since I was a tot. For several years now I have carried this holiday tradition into Colorado by baking these cookies with my good friends, the Slavsky's, whose 3 children count on my arrival each December to bake and decorate hundreds of cookies.

Dough:
1 pound margarine
4 tablespoons sweet cream
1 pound powdered sugar
3 eggs
2-3 tablespoons lemon juice
1 teaspoon baking soda
5-6 cups flour

Frosting:
1 pound powdered sugar
¼ teaspoon salt
¼ cup milk
1 teaspoon vanilla
⅓ cup butter

Cream sugar and margarine. Dissolve the baking soda in lemon juice and add to the sugar and margarine mixture. Mix in the remaining ingredients, with the flour last, adding enough to stiffen the dough. Refrigerate for 1 to 2 hours or even overnight. Roll the dough out on a floured surface to about ¼ inch thickness and cut with your favorite cookie cutters. Bake at 350 degrees on an ungreased cookie sheet for approximately 8 minutes per batch, or until edges begin to brown slightly. Cool on a wire rack. Frost when completely cool.

To make the frosting, beat ingredients together with an electric mixer or food processor. Divide the frosting mixture and add food colorings as desired. Makes approximately 5 dozen.

— Dianne Chrismer

❄ ❄ ❄

'Now, Dasher!

now, Dancer!

now, Prancer

and Vixen!

On, Comet!

on, Cupid!

on, Donder

and Blitzen!

To the top of the

porch, to the top

of the wall!

Now, dash away,

dash away,

dash away all!'

Nana's Cookies

Sand tarts, pecan sandies, Russian Tea cakes…these cookies are called different things by many people. The recipes may vary slightly, but they all contain nuts and are covered with powdered sugar. This particular recipe has been a cherished family favorite for generations. — [Ed.]

1 cup butter
½ cup sugar
2 cups flour, sifted
2 teaspoons vanilla
1 tablespoon water
2 cups pecans, broken
powdered sugar for rolling

Cream butter and sugar. Mix in flour, vanilla, and water. Add pecans and roll into logs about 1½ inches long. Bake at 325 degrees for 25 minutes, or until the bottom edges just begin to brown. While the cookies are still hot and on the cookie sheet, sprinkle liberally and roll in powdered sugar. The heat will make the sugar stick. After cooling, pack between sheets of waxed paper in an air-tight container. Makes 3 dozen.

— Willie Mae Rogers

Eggnog Cookies

My sister, Becky, shared this recipe with me many years ago. My family likes the subtle eggnog flavor.

Cookies:
3 cups flour
¼ teaspoon salt
2 teaspoons nutmeg
1 cup margarine
¾ cup sugar
1 egg
2 teaspoons rum extract
2 teaspoons vanilla extract

Frosting:
⅓ cup margarine
2 teaspoons rum extract
1 teaspoon vanilla
2 cups powdered sugar
2 teaspoons cream or milk

Cream margarine and sugar; add flavorings and beat. Add remaining ingredients. Mix well. Form into logs or balls, then roll in sugar. Bake at 350 degrees for 15 to 18 minutes. Cool, then frost tops and dust with extra nutmeg. Makes 4 dozen.

— Susan Grupe

Kris Kringles

In early December we make hundreds of Scandinavian cookies, which we love to share with friends and family throughout the Christmas season. One family tradition is a "Kris Kringle" cookie which has been passed down from my grandmother.

1 cup shortening
½ cup sugar
2 egg yolks
2 tablespoons grated orange peel
2 teaspoons grated lemon peel
2 teaspoons lemon juice
2 cups flour
1 pinch salt
2 egg whites, slightly beaten
1 cup nuts, finely chopped
candied red and green cherries

Mix the first eight ingredients into a dough. Roll into small balls. Dip each ball in egg white, then nuts. Put a slice of cherry in center of each cookie and press down slightly. Bake at 325 degrees about 20 minutes, or until nuts are toasted. Makes 4 to 5 dozen.

— Karen Helling MacCarter

After baking our Christmas cookies and breads, we deliver them to friends and family.

— S.C., Evergreen

Our dream for a perfect Colorado Christmas would be to have all of our children and their families come home for Christmas!

—V.C., Burlington

And then in a twinkling I heard on the roof The prancing and pawing of each little hoof, As I drew in my head and was turning around, Down the chimney Saint Nicholas came with a bound.

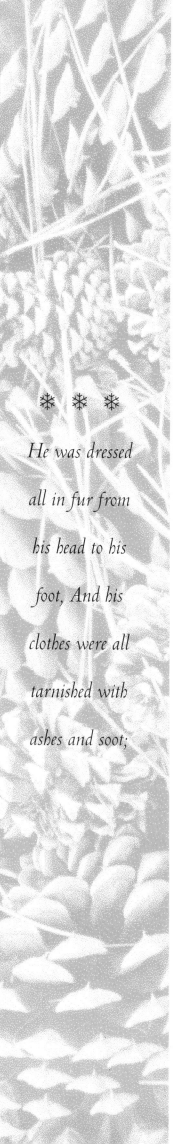
Fudge Bill Likes!

My son-in-law *loves* this fudge—so much that we named it for him!

4 cups sugar
1 12-ounce can evaporated milk
1 stick margarine or butter
1 pinch salt
1 cup semi-sweet chocolate chips

1¼ cups milk chocolate chips
1 7-ounce jar marshmallow creme
2 teaspoons vanilla
2 teaspoons rum
2 cups pecans, chopped

Butter a 3-quart oblong glass baking dish. Place sugar, milk, butter, and salt in a heavy pan on the burner. Turn heat to high and stir while cooking for 10 to 12 minutes or until soft ball stage is reached. It is better to test for soft ball stage, since a candy thermometer can be misleading at high altitudes.

Add chocolate chips and continue cooking until the chocolate is melted. Turn off heat and add marshmallow creme, pecans, and flavorings. Stir until candy begins to get stiff. Pour immediately into prepared pan. Place pan on a rack, not directly on the counter, and let stand overnight.

Cut fudge into small squares and keep in air-tight container with waxed paper between layers. Note: If you like peanut butter fudge, omit the pecans and add 1 cup of peanut butter when you add the marshmallow creme. Makes approximately 6 dozen pieces.

— Frances Ellen Hewitt

Overnight Meringue Cookies

Since these cookies are left overnight, it's great to put them in the oven just before going to bed.

2 egg whites
½ teaspoon cream of tartar
¾ cup sugar
1 6-ounce package mini chocolate, mint, or butterscotch chips
a few drops of food coloring (optional)
a few drops of extract to complement chips, such as rum,
    peppermint, vanilla, or almond
½ cup chopped nuts (optional)

Heat oven to 375 to 400 degrees for at least 15 minutes. Whip egg whites until soft peaks form. Add cream of tartar, sugar, food coloring, and flavoring. Fold in chips and nuts. Drop teaspoonfuls onto greased cookie sheets. Place in oven. Close door and turn off oven. DO NOT OPEN THE OVEN DOOR. Leave cookies in the oven overnight. Remove and store in sealed containers. Makes 2 dozen.

— Dianne Lindenmeyer

❆ ❆ ❆

A bundle of toys

he had flung

on his back,

And he looked like

a pedlar just

opening his pack.

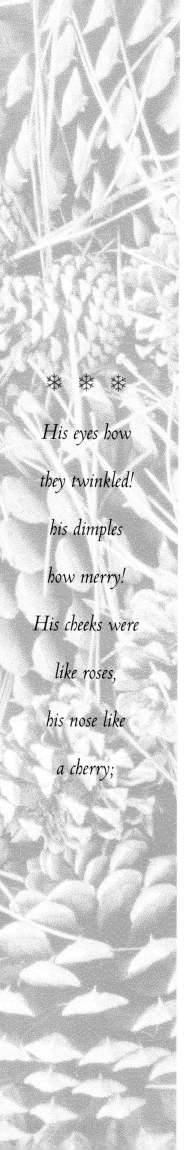

His eyes how

they twinkled!

his dimples

how merry!

His cheeks were

like roses,

his nose like

a cherry;

Gingerbread Treats

Gingerbread cookie ornaments are as much fun to make as they are to eat. This recipe combines several traditional versions and is especially good for "dunking." Little helpers can shape the clay-like dough, or the dough can be rolled out and cut with cookie cutters. Gingerbread men, Christmas trees, Santas, and stars are favorite shapes to decorate and personalize for cookie ornaments. For Golden Girl, pictured here, a gingerbread "dog bone" hangs on her family's tree to include her in the celebration.

Gingerbread Cookies

Dough:

½ cup butter	2½ cups flour
½ cup sugar	½ teaspoon salt
½ cup molasses	½ teaspoon soda
¼ cup water	¾ teaspoon ground ginger

Cream the butter and sugar. Add the molasses and water and mix well. Sift the remaining dry ingredients together and then add gradually to the molasses mixture. Roll the dough into a ball and chill in the refrigerator at least 2 hours.

Prepare the cookie sheet by lining it with aluminum foil. Then mix together ½ cup flour, ¼ cup sugar and 1 to 2 teaspoons cinnamon. Use this mixture to flour the rolling pin and surface. Roll out the cookies to ¼-inch thickness, thicker for larger cookie shapes. A straw makes a perfect hole for hanging if used before baking. Bake the cookies at 375 degrees for about 10 minutes. These may be enjoyed plain or iced. Makes 2½ dozen small cookies.

Icing:

1 tablespoon butter
1½ cup confectioners sugar
¼ cup canned skim milk

Mix the above ingredients. For a thicker consistency add more sugar. Use the icing to decorate your ginger bread cookies; add raisins or red hots for accent.

White Fruit Cake

This recipe is very old and originally had over two quarts of pecans in it. Over the years it has been cut in half twice and now makes one large loaf pan. It can be doubled to make a five-pound cake which fits in a round tube pan.

1 stick butter	½ pound candied cherries, chopped
1 cup sugar	½ pound candied pineapple, chopped
3 egg whites	½ cup apple juice
2 cups flour	1½ teaspoons pure vanilla extract
1 teaspoon baking powder	2 cups pecans, chopped

Cream together butter and sugar, then add the eggs. Sift together flour and baking powder, and mix into butter mixture. Add remaining ingredients. Bake at 300 degrees for about 2½ hours. Cook for less time if using small loaf pans. Place a pan of water on bottom rack of oven to help keep the cake moist while baking. Makes 1 loaf.

—Willie Mae Rogers

❄ ❄ ❄

His droll little mouth was drawn up like a bow, And the beard on his chin was as white as the snow.

In the early 1970s our family tradition of decorating candy houses was started by "Aunt Fran." From that beginning more than twenty years ago, this holiday event has now grown to include a dozen children as well as a few others slightly older!

We were delighted to learn that this Christmas tradition is also an annual custom for others, including the Eklund family from Vail.

To Make a Candy House:

Frosting:

3 pounds powdered sugar

9 egg whites

Beat sugar and egg whites for 20 minutes.

Suggestions for decorations:

candy canes—fences or doorways

red licorice twists—roof edges

chocolate candy bars—doors, windows, walk-ways

Life Savers—wreaths

striped gum—curtains, shutters

M & M's—walks, rocks, flowers

sugar ice cream cones—inverted for Christmas trees

marshmallows—snowmen, snowballs, snow forts

spearmint leaves—shrubs

chocolate cookies—roof shingles

shredded wheat—grass roof shingles

red hots

silver beads

colored sugar sprinkles

assorted hard candies

❄ ❄ ❄

The stump of a

pipe he held tight

in his teeth,

And the smoke it

encircled his head

like a wreath.

Things that make our Christmas special are the candlelight service at church, the Advent wreath, Christmas dinner, and making candy houses!
— K.D., Englewood

Eklund Family Candy House Party

One of our favorite Christmas traditions is to make candy houses with family and friends. We have a party where we serve hot glogg and apple cider, play Christmas music, and the children make candy houses.

Each child is given a cardboard frame for the house, a bowl of frosting, and a bowl of assorted candies. We tape the house frame to a round cardboard base saved from pizzas. The children then cover the houses with frosting and decorate them with candy.

It's fun to see how each individual child creates a holiday house. In addition to enjoying the finished candy house in your own home, they also make nice donations to raffles, hospitals, or needy families.

— Pelle and Chris Eklund, Vail

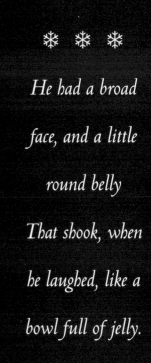

❄ ❄ ❄

He had a broad face, and a little round belly That shook, when he laughed, like a bowl full of jelly.

Skiing home, White River National Forest

A Crystal Farm Christmas typifies the dream many of us have of spending the holidays in the mountains with our families and friends. Getting ready for Christmas is a major undertaking and always more fun when lots of people help.

A Crystal Farm Christmas

Crystal Farm is the historic old ranch at Redstone Castle, in Redstone. It is nestled at the base of towering red cliffs that glisten with massive "icicles," just like nature's own Christmas spectacular. The farm is home to many who come here throughout the year and who gather together for the holiday festivities.

Each Thanksgiving all of the "adopted kids," considered "family" since their early college days in Boulder, gather at the farm. They make the trek into the mountains to find the perfect Christmas trees for the farm celebration. Not just any will do! One tree is for inside the house and the other is for outside. The outside tree seems to get progressively taller each year as the "kids" get older. Now they're not satisfied unless it reaches the peak of the two-story farmhouse!

This trek requires snowmobiles to get to the high mountain property owned by the family. After the trees are cut, everyone gathers in the cabin on top of the mountain for mulled wine and hot chocolate, huddling for warmth around the old cookstove before the long haul back down.

Then we begin the process of building a framework to hold the outside tree. The old backhoe raises it up, and we string the tree with lights. It all ends with a big Thanksgiving dinner to kick off the lighting of the tree.

The inside tree must wait, of course, until the weekend before Christmas when everyone gathers again to cut greens and make wreaths. The pine cones gathered on the mountain in the fall are made into decorations. Ornaments for the tree are handmade by a neighbor—an exquisite collection of porcelain-like angels created from Wonder bread and glue with intricate bouquets of flowers.

Christmas is for all family and friends who need a home away from home. They gather around the twelve-foot table that sits under the deer-antler chandelier, both made on the farm. Fires burn in the hearths of the old farmhouse. Over the main fireplace hangs a hand-carved wooden deer head wreathed in evergreens to celebrate the season.

— Joan Benson & Stephen Kent, Redstone

❄ ❄ ❄

He was chubby and plump, a right jolly old elf, And I laughed when I saw him, in spite of myself. A wink of his eye and a twist of his head Soon gave me to know I had nothing to dread.

While our homes are still decorated for the season and our friends and family are near, we like to toast the arrival of the new while remembering the past. The menu below is appropriate at any time during the holidays, but it's especially festive for ringing in the New Year. This buffet includes several delicious appetizers as well as sweets.

❄ ❄ ❄

He spoke not a

word, but went

straight to his

work, And filled

all the stockings;

then turned

with a jerk,

Open House Buffet

Asparagus Rolls*
Cinnamon Baked Brie
Chafing Dish Meatballs*
Olive Spread with Crackers
Teriyaki Chicken Skewers*
Spinach Mornay Dip
Shrimp Butter for Canapes*
Strawberries Dipped in Chocolate
Bourbon and Rum Balls

* Check Recipe Index for listing.

Asparagus Rolls

This recipe came from a friend named Ann. It has been and still is one of the all-time favorite appetizers that I serve.

Filling:
8 ounces cream cheese, softened
6 to 8 slices bacon, fried crisp
2 tablespoons mayonnaise
garlic powder to taste
⅓ cup pecans, finely chopped
2 green onions, minced

Other ingredients:
12 to 14 slices very fresh white bread
1 stick butter, melted
12 to 14 stalks fresh asparagus, steamed until very tender (Note: canned asparagus can be used when fresh are not in season.)
½ cup parmesan cheese, grated

Mix ingredients for the filling in food processor and set aside. Remove crusts from bread and roll with rolling pin until thin. Spread with filling and place one asparagus stalk inside. Roll up, cut into thirds at a diagonal, and place on baking sheet with seam side down. Brush with melted butter and sprinkle liberally with parmesan cheese. Bake in a 375-degree oven until light brown and crisp, about 20 minutes. Makes 36 to 42 bite-size pieces.

— Fran Strange

Shrimp Butter for Canapes

This may be used as a spread, to stuff cherry tomatoes, or as a filling in the asparagus roll recipe listed above. — [Ed.]

2 6½-ounce cans shrimp, washed and drained
¼ cup onion, grated
8 ounces cream cheese
¾ to 1 cup butter (no substitution)
4 heaping tablespoons Miracle Whip (no substitution)
3 tablespoons fresh lemon juice, to taste

Place all ingredients in food processor and mix.

❄ ❄ ❄

And laying his finger aside of his nose, And giving a nod, up the chimney he rose.

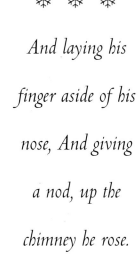

Chafing Dish Meatballs

These meatballs do not need to be cooked before adding the sauce. They also freeze well. — [Ed.]

Meatballs:
2 pounds lean ground beef
1 package dry onion soup mix
3 eggs

Sauce:
12 ounces chili sauce
12 ounces bottled water
1 cup light brown sugar, packed loosely
1 cup sauerkraut, drained and finely chopped
1 16-ounce can whole cranberry sauce

Mix the ingredients for the meatballs and form into small, one-inch balls. Place in baking dish and set aside. Mix the sauce ingredients and place over low heat on the stove top. Simmer until bubbly, about 20 minutes. Pour over meatballs in baking dish. Bake in 350-degree oven for 45 minutes. Serve in chafing dish with cocktail toothpicks. Makes approximately 3 to 4 dozen meatballs.

— Libby Cottingham

Teriyaki Chicken Skewers

This teriyaki sauce can be used on chicken or beef. Everyone loves it! — [Ed.]

Marinade:
½ cup soy sauce
3 tablespoons honey
2 tablespoons vinegar
1½ teaspoons ginger
¼ cup salad oil
2 cloves garlic, crushed
4 green onions with tops, chopped

Pour marinade over 2 pounds of chicken cut into bite-size pieces and set in refrigerator overnight. Skewer and broil, 3 to 4 minutes each side. Makes approximately 20 cocktail skewers.

— Mary Jean Weigel

He sprang to his

sleigh, to his team

gave a whistle,

And away they

all flew like the

down of a thistle;

Christmas celebrations last through January 6th, or Twelfth Night, when the visit of the Magi is commemorated. In most parts of the country, Twelfth Night marks the traditional end of the Christmas season. Many Coloradans, however, consider the last day of the National Western Stock Show & Rodeo in January as the official end of the holiday season.

A Nancarrow Family Twelfth Night Celebration

Twelfth Night, January 6th, is a time for friends to gather and reflect on the events of the past year and to celebrate the prospects of the year ahead. The holiday is said to mark the arrival of the Magi in Bethlehem. On the liturgical calendar, it is an evening of merriment with a similar relationship to Epiphany that Fat Tuesday holds to Ash Wednesday.

Typically, Twelfth Night is an evening for adults and is a time to wear one's holiday finery—tuxedos and sequins are appropriate. Guests are asked to bring an hors d'oeuvre, a gift-wrapped Christmas tree ornament to exchange, and a small branch from their own Christmas tree, distinguished by a bit of ribbon.

When all the guests are assembled and the hors d'oeuvres consumed, the host invites all to partake of the wassail bowl, with one of the guests asked to propose a toast. A King and Queen of Twelfth Night are then selected through a random process to reign for the next several hours.

Paper crowns are bestowed on the royalty, seldom husband and wife, and all guests are required, thereafter, to do their bidding. The agenda for the rest of the evening is prompted by the host and hostess through the King and Queen. The first royal command is for the guests to be seated for dinner, which usually includes the following traditional menu items:

Turkey Chowder
(to symbolize the last use of the holiday bird)
Crusty French Bread
Spinach and Apple Salad
Tipsy Pudding
Wine and Coffee

Following dinner and dessert, the royal couple commands the guests to adjourn to the living room where entertainment is provided by either the guests, if previously asked to do so, or by the host and hostess. At some of our Twelfth Night celebrations, we have adopted a theme and planned the entertainment accordingly.

When the King and Queen have been entertained to their satisfaction, the guests all join in the singing of three or four Christmas carols. The evening draws to a close with each couple carrying the bough from their Christmas tree to the fireplace, sharing a New Year's wish, and then tossing the bough into the fire where it blazes brightly.

Twelfth Night concludes with the host or hostess offering a prayer for the whole group and the singing of Auld Lang Syne.

— Cliff & Debi Nancarrow, Gunnison

But I heard him exclaim, ere he drove out of sight: 'Happy Christmas to all, and to all a good-night!'

Nordic skiing to Gothic, near Crested Butte

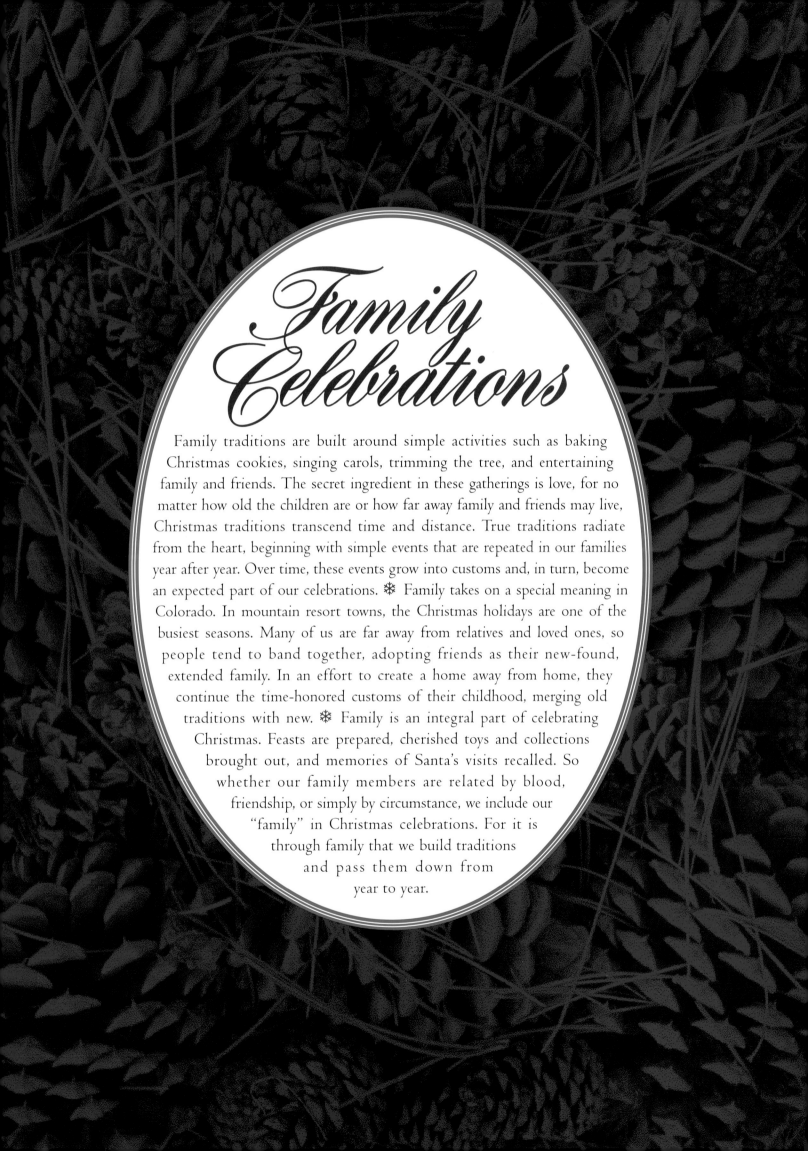

Family Celebrations

Family traditions are built around simple activities such as baking Christmas cookies, singing carols, trimming the tree, and entertaining family and friends. The secret ingredient in these gatherings is love, for no matter how old the children are or how far away family and friends may live, Christmas traditions transcend time and distance. True traditions radiate from the heart, beginning with simple events that are repeated in our families year after year. Over time, these events grow into customs and, in turn, become an expected part of our celebrations. ❅ Family takes on a special meaning in Colorado. In mountain resort towns, the Christmas holidays are one of the busiest seasons. Many of us are far away from relatives and loved ones, so people tend to band together, adopting friends as their new-found, extended family. In an effort to create a home away from home, they continue the time-honored customs of their childhood, merging old traditions with new. ❅ Family is an integral part of celebrating Christmas. Feasts are prepared, cherished toys and collections brought out, and memories of Santa's visits recalled. So whether our family members are related by blood, friendship, or simply by circumstance, we include our "family" in Christmas celebrations. For it is through family that we build traditions and pass them down from year to year.

Telluride Orphan's Christmas

Our tradition is the Annual Telluride Orphan's Christmas Eve Dinner. In Telluride, the majority of the people are far away from their families. And because the holidays are peak season in a ski resort town, it is difficult for most people to get enough time off to visit their families at Christmas.

The annual Telluride Orphan's Christmas Eve Dinner began in 1983. It's a very traditional event with a very traditional dinner. We have Christmas stockings and decorations, a big tree, and presents for everyone. Christmas music is played throughout the evening.

Dinner is usually served buffet style. It used to be a sit-down dinner, but now we are nearly 30 people! After dinner we hand out presents to everyone. Some leave around 11 p.m. to attend midnight mass at the local Catholic church.

On Christmas Day those who don't have to work go skiing, and we gather for a dinner of leftovers that night.

— Ruthann Russell, Telluride

A Creede Christmas for the Neffs

In the beginning of the century, around 1905 to 1929, a miner and his wife raised three sons in a log cabin above Creede. The miner worked his silver mine on the mountainside near his cabin while the sons hiked to school, or skied if it was winter, carrying snow shoes on their backs for the uphill hike home. They hunted and fished for their meat much of the time. Sometimes, they had trap lines to make extra money because the mother lode proved elusive to the miner. He never found it, but he did find a beautiful life high in the San Juan Mountains with his wife and sons.

Christmas was a special time for this family. They didn't have a lot of extras. Their cabin was simple with no electricity or running water, and it was heated by a woodburning stove. On Christmas Eve, the three boys went to bed as usual, with the cabin looking the same as it did on any day.

After the boys were asleep, the miner and his wife would go up on the mountain and chop down a fir tree and carry it back to the cabin. Sometimes this would be quite a chore because there might be a foot and a half of snow. The tree would have to be shaken out and dried.

While the boys slept, the couple decorated the tree with tinsel, glass balls, and little candles in tiny tin candle holders. Then they would set out the gifts by the tree.

There would be something for each boy, always sports or outdoor equipment, like a new hunting knife, fishing pole, or a baseball. One very special Christmas, there were two little trees, both decorated, with a pup tent strung up between and new skis crossed behind it.

Last, and most memorable of all, the miner, in the wee hours of Christmas morning, would go to the

---

Our family trims a live evergreen tree, and we invite someone who might otherwise be alone on Christmas Day.

— V.J., Ouray

We always try to invite others over who would otherwise be alone. It is a great way to have a bit of "family."

— P.D., Aurora

We neither one came to our marriage with any traditions, so we have developed our own over the past 28 years and our children have carried them on!

— J.K., Golden

kitchen, fire up the stove and make crystal, snowy white Divinity Candy that he would roll out into a special sugary treat for Christmas Day. By the time everything was in place under the tree, it was sometimes almost morning; but it truly seemed to the boys that Santa had indeed come.

Old cabin, San Juan Mountains

One of the boys who grew up with those beloved memories learned to make Divinity and became the candymaker for his family. Every Christmas he would make the same wonderful Divinity for his three daughters, who loved it and came to cherish it as their own Christmas tradition. His girls grew up and had families of their own and he made candy for his grandchildren.

Two years ago he died and Christmas wasn't the same without him. For the first time in a long, long time, there was no Divinity Candy at Christmastime.

Then last Christmas, one of the older grandsons brought an unexpected present to the homes of his mother and two aunts. He presented each one with a roll of the Divinity he had made, just like his grandfather's, just like his great grandfather's.

It was the best Christmas present ever!

— Alfred M. Neff, Creede
Beatrice Neff Trautman, Morrison

Our favorite traditions are to open one present on Christmas Eve, the rest on Christmas Day. We eat dinner in the living room by the tree, and we still leave cookies for Santa!

— A.D., Denver

The Neff Family's Divinity Candy

3 cups granulated sugar
½ cup light corn syrup
¾ cup water
1 teaspoon vanilla
½ teaspoon salt
¼ cup egg whites, approximately 2 eggs
1 cup chopped pecans (optional)

Combine sugar, corn syrup, and water in a sauce pan with a good fitting lid. Cook over low heat, stirring until sugar is dissolved. Increase heat and bring to a boil. Then cover and boil without stirring for three minutes. Uncover, insert candy thermometer, and cook evenly until thermometer reaches 265 degrees. In Denver use 250 degrees, and even lower at higher elevations. If you don't have a candy thermometer, cook mixture till it reaches hard ball stage. Remove from heat.

Add salt and vanilla to egg whites; whip by hand or with electric beater at high speed until stiff. Slowly beat in hot syrup, pouring a thin stream from a height of one foot above the egg whites. Continue beating until the mixture almost holds its shape, but is still glossy. This can be tested by allowing a small amount to run from a spoon into the bowl.

If desired, stir in nuts, then pour into a 6-inch square pan lined with waxed paper. Spread lightly into place. Cool and cut into 1½ inch squares. Makes 24 squares.

Try the following variations for something different:

Chocolate Divinity

Use the same recipe and stir in 3 ounces of unsweetened chocolate, melted and cooled, instead of nuts.

Peanut Butter Divinity Roll

Use the basic recipe, but beat until mixture just holds a peak. Place two strips of waxed paper on a board or table; spread a thin coating of butter on the paper and on a rolling pin. Spoon the candy in a ridge across the waxed paper, about 12 inches long and 2 to 3 inches wide. Roll with rolling pin to flatten out like pie dough, to a thickness of ⅛ to ¼ inch and about 20 inches square. Immediately spread 1/16 to ⅛ inch of peanut butter all over candy. Take hold of one edge of the waxed paper and pull it back over the candy to form a roll. Leave waxed paper on candy roll until cool, but not cold. Unwrap and cut into ½-inch slices with warm knife.

Christmas Eve is for family presents, Christmas Day is for Santa's presents.

*— D.N.,
Manitou Springs*

Children bring a sense of anticipation to Christmas. Many of us can remember the long days and never-ending nights just before Santa visits.

When my sisters and I were small we used to have great fun during the holidays. We would tie large leather straps with big bells on them around our waists. As we tore around the house we would sing our favorite Christmas carol, "Rudolph the Red Nosed Reindeer." We would get down on our hands and knees and gallop around, jingling merrily. It was so much fun!

— Shannon Kennedy, age 13, Englewood

Listening to special Christmas music, putting out cookies and milk for Santa and carrots for the reindeer, then going to sleep to wait for Santa.

— The H. Family, Westminster

Spending the holidays with our parents, and as many family members as possible. We eat macaronis—all kinds!

— R.R., Pueblo

Opening one present on Christmas Eve.

— S.W.P., Basalt

Looking forward to my grandmother's coffee cake on Christmas morning!

— S.V., Boulder

Singing carols while someone plays the piano or organ. The children tell what they liked about the last year.

— G.H., Aurora

Visiting old friends—or having old friends visit us!

— F.C., Parker

Spending Christmas Eve at Grandmother's house and Christmas Day at home.

— B.P., Englewood

Opening our gifts on Christmas morning, but we have a special husband and wife gift exchange on Christmas Eve after the children are asleep.

— C.J., Denver

Celebrating Christmas on the 24th and looking forward to midnight "mess."

— T.S., Littleton

Grand Lake Lodge Eggnog

This special recipe has been used for years to celebrate Christmas in August by the staff of the Grand Lake Lodge. I serve it in an antique hand-painted china punch bowl with a silver ladle.

12 eggs, separated
6 tablespoons sugar
2 pints whole milk
½ pint whipping cream
1 pint liquor (⅔ bourbon and ⅓ rum or brandy), optional

Beat yolks until lemon color. Add sugar, beating until dissolved. Add liquor slowly until eggs are "cooked." Whip egg whites until stiff; whip the cream separately. Add egg whites and cream alternately to yolk mixture to make a frothy beverage. Sprinkle fresh grated nutmeg on top. Makes 20 four-ounce servings.

— Bob Scott

Colorado Christmas Eve dinners reflect Victorian influences brought here during the late 1800s when the state was being settled. Roast beef was mentioned most frequently as an entree. This Christmas Eve menu tastefully expresses the varied foods and western flavor of the region.

Christmas Eve Dinner

Grand Lake Lodge Eggnog

Western Rib Roast*

Yorkshire Pudding

Horseradish Sauce

Colorado Layered Spinach Salad with Pine Nuts

English Peas and Onions

Christmas Pudding*

* Check Recipe Index for listing.

Western Rib Roast

This western version of a beef roast will delight your family and guests! Tim Luksa, the executive chef at Epicurean Catering in Denver, graciously shares his secrets with us. — [Ed.]

1 15- to 18-pound western rib roast	2 tablespoons each black pepper,
1 tablespoon salt	granulated garlic, fresh rosemary,
	fresh thyme, and fresh marjoram

Trim fat cap from rib. Trim meat and fat up 2 inches from the end of the bone. Your butcher should do these first two tasks for you. Mix seasonings and rub all over the prime rib. Place in roasting pan and roast in preheated 275-degree oven for about 2½ hours. Remove from oven and let rest ½ hour. An internal temperature of 120 degrees will serve a medium rare, after resting out of the oven for 30 minutes. Increase internal temperature by 10 degrees for each level of doneness desired. Serves approximately 30.

— Tim Luksa

Christmas Pudding

This traditional "Figgy Pudding" came from my good friend Sue. We celebrate Christmas together, and this dessert is our families' favorite.

1 cup dried dates, chopped coarse	1½ cups flour
1 cup boiling water	2 tablespoons baking powder
1 egg	½ teaspoon baking soda
1 cup sugar	½ teaspoon salt
½ cup chopped nuts, pecans or walnuts	

Put dried dates and water in food processor and puree. Mix in egg, then add sugar and chopped nuts. Sift together flour, baking powder, baking soda, and salt. Add to liquid mixture. Place in a well-buttered mold and steam for about 1 hour and 15 minutes at 350 degrees. Test for doneness by touching to see if it is set. After it is done, invert onto an oven-safe pan and set aside. DO NOT DOUBLE THE RECIPE. Next make the vanilla sauce.

Vanilla Sauce:

2 sticks butter, melted	2 cups powdered sugar
2 eggs	1½ teaspoons vanilla

Melt butter in a heavy pan over low heat; add sugar and dissolve. Whisk in eggs, being careful they don't curdle. Cook till mixture thickens. Add vanilla last.

Warm pudding slightly if cool at serving time. Garnish with candied cherries or nut halves, then pour on vanilla sauce while it's hot. Pudding will soak up much of the sauce. Serve immediately. Serves 8 generously.

— Margaret Aarestad

On Christmas Day, as families gather to open gifts, many celebrate with a festive breakfast. After an elaborate Christmas Eve dinner the night before, many families enjoy a breakfast or brunch in place of a big Christmas Day dinner. This Christmas breakfast menu features an outstanding apple cake.

Christmas Breakfast

Christmas Egg Strata
Grandma Hill's 3/4 Apple Cake
Fresh Pineapple and Strawberries
Orange Juice
Hot Spiced Tomato Juice*
Vanilla Flavored Coffee

* Check Recipe Index for listing.

Grandma Hill's 3/4 Apple Cake

I usually mix Jonathan and Granny Smith apples; Delicious apples are sweeter. It's wonderful with ice cream!

3 to 4 medium apples, sliced and peeled	¾ stick butter
Cinnamon and sugar	¾ teaspoon baking powder
¾ cup sugar	1 egg
¾ cup flour	⅛ teaspoon salt, optional

Slice the peeled apples into an 8x8-inch buttered pan. Sprinkle with cinnamon and sugar, stirring until all slices are covered. In a separate bowl, mix remaining ingredients; batter will be stiff. Spread it over the top of the apples so none of them are showing. Bake at 350 degrees for ½ to ¾ hour, until crust is golden and apples are bubbly. Serve hot or cold for breakfast, brunch, or dessert. Serves 6 to 8.

— Jan E. Kiefer

For variety, you may add ½ cup cold coffee, ½ cup chopped walnuts, and 1 cup chopped dates to create a moist cake with an interesting texture and flavor. Bake at 375 degrees for ¾ hour. — [Ed.]

Hot Spiced Tomato Juice

This recipe comes from an old friend and has been a favorite winter drink since 1968. Although I have lost touch with her, I think of her every time I drink a warm, soothing cup. Enjoy! — [Ed.]

    4 cups tomato juice
    2 tablespoons catsup
    1 teaspoon salt, or less
    ⅛ teaspoon pepper
    juice of one lemon and rind, grated
    ½ teaspoon Tabasco
    1 tablespoon Worcestershire

Combine all ingredients and bring almost to a boil. Simmer for a few minutes to let flavors blend. Serves 6.

Our "extended" family makes our Christmas special. We always seem to have someone extra at our house. Mother finds gifts for everyone. She doesn't want anyone to be without a present to open on Christmas morning. We have a special breakfast and friends come by and visit all morning on Christmas Day. It is a wonderful day!

— K.H., Telluride

As a family gift, we always select a jigsaw puzzle to put together over the Christmas holidays. As the children got older, the puzzles became more difficult. This tradition started with my husband's family.

— N.L., Englewood

We have a big brunch after we open our gifts.

— G.S., Ft. Collins

On Christmas morning we open our gifts and call all of our out-of-state relatives on the telephone. It is everyone for himself for breakfast, but the main meal is at 1:00 p.m.

— P.D., Aurora

We invite the immediate family plus aunts, uncles, nieces, nephews, cousins, spouses, and grandchildren to congregate at one of our homes for a potluck dinner and to exchange handmade gifts. Each person gives one gift to one other family member. We draw names and set the dollar limit for next year's Christmas gift exchange.

— M.J., Denver

Tamales are our holiday tradition. Our entire family, more than three generations, enjoys making as well as eating them. Their preparation, however, is time consuming, but can be great fun if you have family and friends to help. It takes us about four hours.

— J.T., Denver

Many of our family members are from Colorado, Illinois, and Texas. We gather at the home that holds the most!

— N.I.L., Grand Lake

Christmas morning presents are followed by a big family breakfast of posole and green chili.

— J.Z., Denver

Being together, opening gifts, having a nice midday dinner with people dropping by makes our Christmas Day special.

— D.B., Westminster

Dinner on Christmas Day is truly a feast! Treasured family recipes are prepared and shared. Traditional favorites are roast turkey and baked ham with accompaniments galore. Both stuffing and dressing recipes compete with each other for space on the buffet table. Sweet potatoes and yams are also popular, though few can agree on which is best. The Christmas Day dinner menu listed below reflects a wide variety of Colorado favorites.

Christmas Day Dinner

Relish Tray

Toasted Pecans

Roast Turkey

Baked Ham

Apple Nut Sage Stuffing

Grandmother's Cornbread Dressing*

Sweet Potato Casserole

Mom's Yummy Yams*

Mashed Potatoes and Gravy

Fresh Green Beans

Cranberry Relish*

Cranberry Jello Salad*

Maureen's Snail Rolls*

Pecan Pie*

Pumpkin Pie

Cookie Plate

* Check Recipe Index for listing.

Apple Nut Sage Stuffing

Chef Jim Schlarbaum is chief of operations at Epicurean Catering in Denver. This is his personal recipe which he has generously shared with us. — [Ed.]

1 stick unsalted butter
1 large onion, medium diced
6 stalks celery, medium diced
2 Granny Smith apples, medium diced
2 cloves garlic, minced
1 teaspoon each fresh rosemary, thyme, marjoram and oregano
2 ounces fresh sage
1 teaspoon each fresh black pepper and salt
2 loaves fresh french bread, large cubes
1 pound walnuts, chopped
2 cups turkey stock
2 eggs

Saute vegetables, apples, and spices in butter until onions are transparent. Add to french bread and toss. Add walnuts, stock, and eggs. Mix well. Form into a mounded shape about 14x6 inches; refrigerate until cold. Make your stuffing one day ahead and don't worry if it looks too dry—it will absorb the turkey juices as it cooks. Serves 10 to 12.

— Jim Schlarbaum

Grandmother's Cornbread Dressing

Cornbread dressing is legendary in the South. Because Colorado has so many southerners who have adopted Colorado, we included a recipe reminiscent of that background. Unlike stuffing, cornbread dressing is cooked outside the turkey. This one is easy, and is typical of many treasured family "secret" recipes. — [Ed.]

In order to get this recipe, I had to stand next to my grandmother and watch her prepare it.

½ skillet baked cornbread, crumbled
5 to 6 slices white bread
salt and pepper to taste, about ½ teaspoon each
1 small onion, chopped fine
2 eggs, slightly beaten
2 cups homemade chicken broth
3 stalks celery, chopped fine (optional)

Butter an oven-safe baking dish; use a 9x9-inch or 7x10-inch casserole.

Crumble cooked cornbread in a large bowl. Tear white bread in small pieces and add to cornbread. Soak in chicken broth. Add onion, salt and pepper to taste and then add eggs. Stir to mix. Bake in 350-degree oven for 1½ hours. Serves 6.

This may be doubled or frozen before cooking. If frozen, partially thaw before placing in oven.

— Jean Cooper

Maureen's Snail Rolls

Our holiday tradition includes trading Snail Rolls—my mother's recipe—and pecan pies with my dear friend. We each make a double recipe and then exchange half of the Snail Rolls for a pie. Sometimes we celebrate by eating together, but even if we aren't spending the day together, we take a few minutes to visit.

½ cup milk
2 tablespoons sugar
½ teaspoon salt
¼ cup salad oil
1 egg

1 package yeast
¼ cup warm water
2 cups flour
2 tablespoons melted butter

Scald the milk and add sugar, salt, and oil. Beat egg into mixture. Be sure milk is not too hot. In a small bowl, dissolve in ¼ cup lukewarm water and add to scalded milk mixture. Add flour to liquid and mix well; dough should be sticky. Let rise for two hours, though it may not need this much time in high altitudes.

On a floured board, roll dough into a large circle. Spread with melted butter and cut into 16 pie-shaped wedges. Roll from large end into crescent rolls. Let rise again. Bake on a cookie sheet at 400-425 degrees for 6 to 7 minutes. Watch carefully as they burn easily. This dough can also be filled with cinnamon, nuts, jellies, or brown sugar before rolling into crescents. Makes 16 rolls.

— Maureen Lienert

Mom's Yummy Yams

"Mom" suggested that we double the topping recipe. We didn't know why until we made it. The cooks—and everyone else—kept tasting the topping until we had to make the second recipe just to have some to cover the yams! — [Ed.]

Yam Mixture:
2 cups mashed yams, boiled and skinned
   or 1 40-ounce can, mashed
1 cup white sugar
3 eggs, beaten
⅔ stick butter or margarine
1 cup milk
½ teaspoon nutmeg
½ teaspoon cinnamon
1½ teaspoons vanilla

Topping:
¾ cup corn flakes, crushed
½ cup pecans, broken or crushed
½ cup brown sugar
¾ stick butter, melted

Place all ingredients in a food processor or large mixer and whip. Place in a buttered 9x13-inch baking dish and bake at 400 degrees for 30 minutes.

Mix the topping ingredients together. After the initial cooking time for the yams, remove them from the oven and sprinkle the topping over them. Cook an additional 15 minutes at 400 degrees until sugars begin to caramelize and crust begins to form.

— Therese McClure

Pecan Pie

Good pecans are the secret to making a great pecan pie. To decorate the top, I arrange whole pecans with the ends facing toward the center in concentric circles around the edges of the pie plate. Trust me, this is the best ever!

1 unbaked pie shell, not pricked

Filling:
3 eggs
½ cup sugar
1 cup dark Karo syrup
¼ cup butter, melted (no substitutions)
1 teaspoon vanilla
1½ cups pecans

Beat eggs well. Add sugar and blend. Stir in Karo syrup and melted butter. Add vanilla. Pour into unbaked pie shell. Arrange nuts on top. Bake at 350 degrees for 1 hour.

— Heidi Keogh

We celebrate by having friends over on Christmas Day and Santa visiting the children.

—The M.S. Family,
Carbondale

Christmas Eve we get together with friends, and open gifts on Christmas morning. We wish to have the entire family from all corners of the U.S. come here with their children and grandchildren. My 88-year-old mother still makes our Jello salad every Christmas.

— D.G., Denver

My German grandmother would make homemade noodles and tell us "to be sure to roll them thin enough to read the newspaper through." She always made chicken and noodles for sick neighbors at Christmastime.

— C.W., Brush

Early Colorado settlers valued cranberries because cold weather did not ruin them. Fresh fruits and vegetables were difficult to transport over the high mountain passes for the produce would freeze. While oranges and apples had to be stored in cellars in early fall, cranberries could be shipped by train and wagon throughout the winter months. Cranberries are easily adapted to many recipes, providing color, taste, and vitamins.

Cranberry Jello Salad

Everyone has a favorite Jello recipe, and this one is especially good. — [Ed.]

1 cup raw cranberries, chopped	1 orange with rind, chopped
¼ cup sugar	1 cup celery, chopped
1 package raspberry Jello	1 cup walnuts or pecans, chopped
½ cup hot water	red food coloring
1 cup crushed pineapple with syrup	

Combine cranberries and sugar in food processor, chop coarsely. Let stand a few minutes. Taste and add more sugar, if desired. Add orange and chop again. Dissolve gelatin in hot water. Add pineapple juice, cool, then add crushed pineapple. Add enough red food coloring to make it pretty. Chill until firm. It may be poured into a mold or into a 9x13-inch pan, and cut into squares. If molds are used, grease with mayonnaise before pouring in Jello mixture. If you like firmer Jello, you may add some regular gelatin or use a large package of Jello with ¾ cup of hot water. Serves 12 to 15.

— Frances R. Hewitt

Cranberry Relish

We found this was so good that we would eat it on anything! — [Ed.]

16 ounces cranberries, washed and picked over
2 cups raisins
3½ cups sugar
½ cup white vinegar
1 cup pecans, chopped
½ teaspoon ground cloves

Put all ingredients in a large, heavy saucepan and place on low heat. This does not have a lot of liquid in it when you begin. When it comes to a boil, simmer for 15 minutes. Put in hot sterilized jars or pack in freezer containers. Use as an accompaniment, or place a teaspoonful inside muffins before baking. Also good on fresh or cooked pears and peaches. Makes about 3½ to 4 cups.

— Donna Burns

Cranberry Date Bars

These date bars are featured in the Snow Picnic menu in the Outdoor section. They're not only pretty, but delicious, too! — [Ed.]

Filling:
3 cups fresh cranberries, washed
   and picked over
8 ounces dates, pitted and chopped
¼ cup water
1 teaspoon vanilla

Batter:
2 cups all-purpose flour
2 cups rolled oats
1½ cups brown sugar, packed
½ teaspoon baking soda
¼ teaspoon salt
1 cup margarine or butter, melted

Glaze:
2 cups powdered sugar
2 tablespoons orange juice
½ teaspoon vanilla

Combine filling ingredients, except vanilla, in a medium saucepan. Cover and cook over low heat, stirring frequently, for 10 to 15 minutes or until cranberries pop. Add vanilla. Set filling aside.

Mix batter ingredients. Pat half of the oat mixture into the bottom of a buttered 13x9x2-inch baking pan. Bake in a 350-degree oven for 8 minutes.

Carefully spread filling over baked oat mixture. Sprinkle with the remaining oat mixture. Pat gently. Bake for 20 to 22 minutes more or until golden brown. Cool on a wire rack.

Mix glaze ingredients. Add additional orange juice, 1 teaspoon at a time, to reach drizzling consistency. Drizzle glaze over baked mixture. Cut into bars. Makes 32 date bars.

— Lucy Meyring

On December 24 we open gifts and play games.
   — R.H., Colorado Springs

On Christmas Eve we go to church and light our Advent candles. We wake up very early the next morning and open stockings and presents. In the evening we go to Grandma's house to open presents.
   — B.C., Englewood

*H*istorically many Coloradans have had to spend Christmas Day working. In the early days, people counted on the railroad to run, so for the railroaders, Christmas was just another day. Today, because peak ski season occurs during the holidays, transportation providers and ski resort, hotel, and restaurant employees must all work through the Christmas season. Ranchers, too, must tend to their duties on Christmas Day.

C Lazy U Ranch

A Meyring Kind of Christmas

Being a ranching family and living in rugged country here in North Park, our livestock must be tended every single day throughout the winter months, including Christmas Day. For this reason, our big celebration is on Christmas Eve, when the entire family and several neighbors get together for a delicious meal of prime rib, wild rice casserole, and a medley of vegetables.

After the meal, we all gather around a beautifully decorated tree, which we cut from our own property and decorate differently from year to year with various themes. The patriarch of the family, "Twist," who is now 84 years old, distributes the gifts from under the tree. Everyone is grateful and thankful for the goodness bestowed upon us for another year.

Christmas morning is "just another day," as our cattle have to be fed as always. The men feed and harness their teams of Percheron draft horses and set off on their sleds to feed the cattle. It's brisk and cold, steam rises from the sweating horses and the air sparkles with frost particles. It's truly great to be alive and to be doing what so many people can only dream of!

— Lucy Meyring, Walden

*G*athering at family member's homes for dinner and a gift exchange is how we celebrate Christmas.
— M.T., Fort Collins

North Platte River, North Park

*J*ulia Tapia, a widow and parishioner at Our Lady of Guadalupe Church, has four children, ten grandchildren and two great-grandchildren. In 1944 she moved to Denver, where she raised her family. A story that she wrote for *The Denver Post* in December of 1986, reprinted here with permission, tells how she first came to know Santa Claus. Julia Tapia still makes empanadas for Christmas and still believes in Santa Claus.

Christmas Memories of Santa's First Visit

I don't remember doing much for Christmas until the year I turned seven. It was 1923 and we lived in Vaughn, a small town in New Mexico where children didn't know about things like Santa Claus. Spanish families had different customs in those times.

All that changed one evening in early December. My mother was cooking the evening meal over an old pot-bellied stove in our kitchen when my father came home from his job as a laborer for the railroad.

He changed into a freshly starched shirt and tugged on his familiar dark suspenders. Then, he joined us children at the kitchen table. There were five of us then: my brother Jake was 11, Frances was 9, I was 7, Mela was 5, and Emma was 3.

I remember my father's face that night. He looked tired from the day's work, but his eyes twinkled as if he had a secret he couldn't wait to tell.

After dinner, he got out the Montgomery Ward catalog that my mother used to order material for our clothes. But on this particular night, my father didn't look at cloth. Instead, he turned to the toy section and said we'd better put in our order to Santa Claus.

Well, we didn't even know who Santa Claus was! There was no radio or television in those days to tell children he would come on Christmas if they were good.

My father told us Santa Claus would come down the chimney of the stove on Christmas Eve and leave us presents. We were very happy about this idea. I remember how we all sat at the kitchen table looking at that catalog. We wanted to order everything, but my father laughed and told us to order just one thing each.

Oh, there were so many beautiful things to choose from! Jake wanted a play farm set, and Frances asked for a sewing kit because she liked to embroider. My two younger sisters wanted the same dolls.

But I saw this beautiful porcelain doll with jointed hands and curly brown hair. She even had green eyes made of real marbles that closed so she could sleep. I always wished I had light eyes like my mother's, which were hazel. But mine are dark brown. So, the minute I saw that doll, I knew I wanted her and nothing else.

My father wrote it all down in the letter, and we were so happy. My mother just smiled and shook her head; I don't think she knew much about Santa Claus either.

The weeks before Christmas, I wondered about this Santa Claus. Would he be able to read my father's writing? Would the stove be too hot for him to come down the chimney? Did he know I wanted the doll with the green eyes?

Christmas Eve finally came and we had to keep our own traditions. Because Vaughn was so small, the priest only came once a month, so we couldn't go to Midnight Mass like we do now. But my mother sang "Noche de Paz," and we all joined her in singing "Silent Night" as we bundled up to go ask for *oremos*, an old custom where children go door to door singing in exchange for treats.

Later we made empanadas, stuffed pastries. My father would bring home the coal and the meat. In those days you didn't have oil so we had to use lard. My job was grinding the beef tongue for the filling.

After we finished, all the girls put on the new flannel nightgowns my mother had made us. We all slept in the same room in two double beds. We were so tired from the excitement, but we giggled and worried about whether Santa Claus would really come. We tried to stay awake and wait for him, but then morning came and we'd been sleeping and missed him.

We ran to the living room and saw that what my father told us was true: Santa had come in the night! And there was my beautiful doll!

When I think about my father and how he brought us Santa Claus, I feel so much love for him, just remembering these things and knowing how wonderful he tried to make our childhood.

— Julia Rael Tapia, Denver

Bizcochitos

Bizcochitos are traditional holiday cookies. I use a cookie press and make little Christmas trees.

6 cups flour, sifted
3 teaspoons baking powder
1 teaspoon salt
1 pound lard
½ cup sugar
2 teaspoons anise seed
2 eggs
¼ cup brandy
¼ cup sugar
1 tablespoon cinnamon

Preheat oven to 350 degrees. Sift flour, baking powder and salt. Separately, cream shortening with sugar and anise seeds. Beat eggs until light and fluffy; add to creamed mixture. If desired, add a few drops of food coloring to make red or green cookies. Combine brandy with flour mixture, using enough to form a stiff dough. Knead slightly, roll out to ¼-inch thickness, and cut with cookie cutters. Dust with the sugar and cinnamon mixture. Bake about 8 minutes. Makes 8 to 10 dozen.

— Julia Rael Tapia

*C*ollecting Simpich Character Dolls is a holiday tradition for many Colorado families. These intricately detailed dolls are prized by individuals and collectors from all over the world. Each one is handcrafted, and making them has since grown into a beloved family business. The story of the Simpich Dolls began at Christmastime.

The Story of Simpich Dolls

Simpich Character Dolls

*W*e really enjoy seeing the Simpich marionette version of A Christmas Carol. *It is part of our Christmas tradition.*

— K.Z.,
Colorado Springs

The tale of the Simpich Dolls began in Colorado Springs in the fall of 1952. As newlyweds with a limited budget, we began to plan what we could make for Christmas gifts. We were pleased with the enthusiasm with which the first characters were received when, on Christmas Eve, our parents opened the first set of carolers and a group of peasants. Assuming these to be the first and last of their kind, we were pleasantly surprised when others requested additional figures.

As demand and interest grew, other characters were created. The first angels were added in 1954, and a group of classic storybook characters the following year at the request of the Denver schools. By 1960, the Pilgrims, Cratchits, and Scrooge had been designed and shortly thereafter, the Elves. With the arrival of our third child in 1961, we added the Cloud Babies.

After a time, Bob's job teaching art in the schools, an active family of four children, and the growing doll business created the need for additional helpers. Neighbors, family, and friends took on the tasks of hemming skirts, sewing pants and shoes, twisting the wire frames, and doing other piecework to lighten the load.

At times we have been tempted to go into some kind of mass production, but always arrive at the same conclusions: The charm of our art is the hand touch, and the value is that only a limited number can be made each year.

Because of this, our dolls are in art museums and private collections across the country. We have tried to make them a celebration of life under God.

— Bob and Jan Simpich,
Colorado Springs

Santa's Helpers

For three generations in our family, when the stockings were hung, the Christmas surprises began. My parents agonized over the Santa revelation. As a transition from Santa's presents to grown-up traditions, they decided to include us in the secrets of giving.

As each of us became old enough to make and wrap presents, we "helped" Santa by filling each other's stockings. The gifts were small and often represented family jokes. Later, our spouses and our children were each given their special family stocking.

Whether our Christmases were prosperous or lean, the stocking gifts and their memories, pranks, and family jokes have become the one tradition which we plan for all year long.

— Laura Dirks, Denver

We sit around the fire and talk about the good things that happened during the last year. Sometimes we even send tapes.

— L.W., Grand Junction

Memories of My Grandfathers

My most unforgettable Christmas memory is that of sitting under the huge Christmas tree in the dining room of my grandmother's house, carefully reading the tags on dozens of presents. I was searching for the presents for my grandfathers and putting them aside before Christmas morning. I was nine years old, and both my grandfathers had just passed away.

Everyone was in a general state of disarray and didn't seem to notice how quietly I was doing my assigned task. I had separated a small pile of packages, mostly socks, from the other packages under the tree and was placing them nearby under the dining room table. It was a favorite hiding place for my younger sister and me. We loved to sit for hours and talk while we watched the pretty bubble lights and shiny red balls on the tree just a few feet away. Somehow, I couldn't bring myself to move from under the dining room table. I didn't want anyone to see me sobbing.

We hang socks on Christmas Eve, and open them Christmas morning or at Christmas dinner. The socks are filled with small gifts and little jokes and puzzles.

— B.M.S., Ouray

I can still see the underside of that big oak table in my memories. The lights of the Christmas tree looked so fuzzy and blurred in my tears. It was then that I learned that Christmas could bring both joy and sorrow. The sorrow would fade and slowly turn into fond memories, but the joy remains forever.

I treasure the memory of that special hiding place, the pretty lights, and my grandfathers. And I am thankful that I had a few minutes to remember them in my own way and to begin to understand the true meaning of Christmas.

— Sally Daniel, Englewood

Blizzard of '82

One of my favorite memories is the blizzard of 1982. It was Christmas Eve and we were stranded at the Denver airport and going nowhere fast. The children were getting tired and cranky, therefore making the parents cranky, too. The children were upset about not knowing how Santa would—or could—find them.

There was also a man stranded at the airport who was going home to visit his young son, whom he hadn't seen for some time. He noticed that the children were upset about missing Santa Claus. He went around to the bars on the concourse and collected money and bought all of the popcorn balls and candy canes available at the airport shops.

Later, around 5:30 or 6:00 pm, he went into the men's room and changed. He emerged in the Santa suit that he had planned to wear to surprise his son. He put a chair in the middle of the concourse and invited all of the children to talk with him.

They were so happy to visit with Santa. Each child received a popcorn ball and candy cane with the knowledge that Santa had already taken presents to wherever the child was going.

— Patty L. Stanley, Highlands Ranch

The joy of Christmas is found in giving. In this story the Bird family shows how important and how much fun it can be to include others with thoughtful little gifts at Christmastime.

The Bird Family
Twelve Days of Christmas Tradition

Each year, beginning on December 13, our family (two parents and five children) anonymously delivers daily gifts with a "Twelve Days of Christmas" theme to a carefully selected family. The gifts vary yearly as our creative juices ebb and flow, but some of the traditional ones include: two turtle doves (two bars of Dove soap with chocolate turtles taped on top), three French hens (three freshly baked loaves of French bread shaped liked hens), five golden rings (five doughnuts), eight maids a'milking (eight small cartons of milk), ten lords a'leaping (ten gingerbread men with legs in leaping positions), and twelve drummers (twelve fried chicken drumsticks).

We try to choose families who are new to the area and have small children or families who might need cheering up for any number of reasons. The family we deliver gifts to begins to anticipate our nightly arrivals, and the ring-and-run challenge becomes more and more difficult. But we've found ways to stump them. Sometimes we deliver the gifts before dawn or deliberately have someone else knock on the door and hand them a gift just to throw them off.

On the final day, Christmas Eve, we conclude the gift giving by caroling at the chosen home. Of course, we sing "The Twelve Days of Christmas." That's when the mystery is unraveled and our two families trade stories about close calls and happy hunches.

Sometimes it's been difficult to prepare gifts every day during those already extra busy days just before Christmas, but we wouldn't give it up for anything. This tradition has encouraged us to extend ourselves to others in a fun way. It's been good for us and our Twelve Days families.

One mother has told us repeatedly in the years since her family was chosen that our gift giving was the only thing that got her through the holidays. Her husband had died of cancer just before Thanksgiving that year, and she didn't have the emotional energy to make Christmas a happy one for her children. Our twelve days of gift giving filled the gap. We've been close friends ever since.

—The Richard and Twila Bird Family,
Lakewood

Christmas is a special time of just being together, decorating, cooking, and participating in church Christmas programs. Our cul-de-sac decorates their houses based on a Twelve Days of Christmas theme.

— S.E., Englewood

Simpich Character Dolls

Overlooking Georgetown

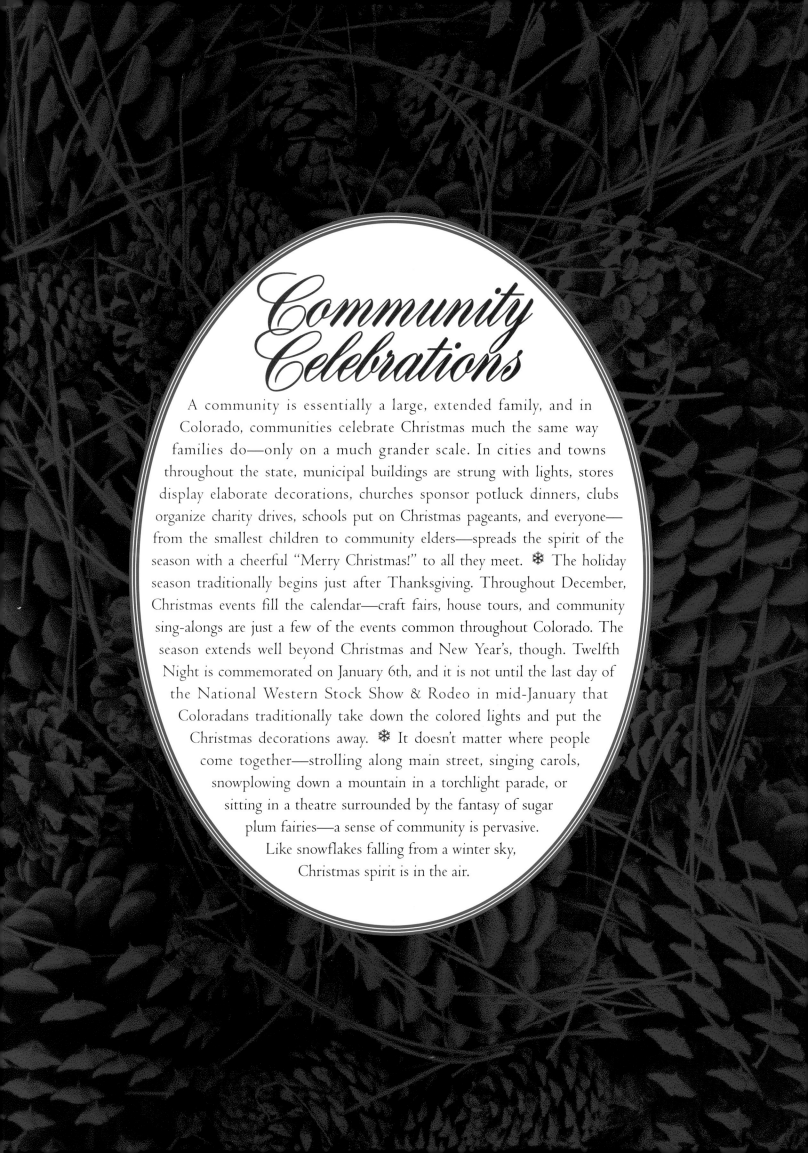

Community Celebrations

A community is essentially a large, extended family, and in Colorado, communities celebrate Christmas much the same way families do—only on a much grander scale. In cities and towns throughout the state, municipal buildings are strung with lights, stores display elaborate decorations, churches sponsor potluck dinners, clubs organize charity drives, schools put on Christmas pageants, and everyone—from the smallest children to community elders—spreads the spirit of the season with a cheerful "Merry Christmas!" to all they meet. ❋ The holiday season traditionally begins just after Thanksgiving. Throughout December, Christmas events fill the calendar—craft fairs, house tours, and community sing-alongs are just a few of the events common throughout Colorado. The season extends well beyond Christmas and New Year's, though. Twelfth Night is commemorated on January 6th, and it is not until the last day of the National Western Stock Show & Rodeo in mid-January that Coloradans traditionally take down the colored lights and put the Christmas decorations away. ❋ It doesn't matter where people come together—strolling along main street, singing carols, snowplowing down a mountain in a torchlight parade, or sitting in a theatre surrounded by the fantasy of sugar plum fairies—a sense of community is pervasive. Like snowflakes falling from a winter sky, Christmas spirit is in the air.

Christmas in Craig

The observance of the Christmas season in the town of Craig demonstrates the power of community spirit. It is a time when all are helpful, cooperative, and considerate of others.

On the Saturday after Thanksgiving, businesses decorate their establishments with lights and delightful Christmas displays. The town arranges for street decorations according to a theme selected by the chamber of commerce.

Homeowners also decorate the outside of their houses, which adds to the festive spirit.

On a designated night, a committee judges all the decorated houses and commercial establishments. The winners are rated first, second, third, and special mention, but no prizes are given out—the honor is in the recognition. Transportation is provided so shut-ins and the elderly can see the lights and decorations, creating a special event for all to enjoy.

Santa, of course, shows up in the stores to have his picture taken with children and to listen to their Christmas wishes for gifts. A Santa suit is also available at the chamber of commerce office for use by other would-be Santas.

During the past several years toys have been collected at various locations around town for a "Toys for Tots" campaign. Toys needing mending are repaired by volunteers. Last year the National Guard, assisted by the Lions Club, collected and distributed these gifts to needy children and teenagers. The Elks Lodge usually provides for the children, too; sometimes it is a movie in the afternoon with candy for every child.

There are approximately twenty women who volunteer at the Food Bank. This past year they put together 175 baskets of food for needy families. Small families received $5 for the purchase of meat, while larger families received $10. This money came from the United Way, with other funds and food donations from individuals, clubs, and organizations, including the Boy Scouts and Craig Middle School students.

Churches have their special observations of Christmas. One particular event is when the singers from the various church choirs join together for a cantata. This outstanding performance always draws large crowds.

The Parade of Lights is another event which receives a lot of attention. On the Saturday following Thanksgiving, whoever wants to participate decorates floats for the Christmas season, following a theme selected by the Lions Club. A grand marshall is chosen and prizes are awarded for floats. The parade route goes through downtown, passing rest homes and senior citizens' residences. The Parade of Lights is exciting for everyone, especially on a snowy night.

There are also many Christmas parties throughout town hosted by individuals, clubs, organizations, and businesses to celebrate the season with their members, employees, friends, and customers. Contributions are often collected for the needy at these affairs, but best of all are the fellowship and good wishes expressed by each individual. And as they say to each other, so say we to you. Merry Christmas!

— Elsie B. Wingo, Craig

*T*hroughout the state, Coloradans look forward to classic holiday performances. Plays, ballets, and musical productions reflect the informal flavor of Colorado living and are interwoven into the fabric of our community celebrations. From theatre stages to high school auditoriums and church halls, beloved Christmas stories evoke the magic of the season.

U.S. Air Force Academy

J *ust after Thanksgiving, at the United States Air Force Academy in Colorado Springs, a 90-member cadet chorale performs Handel's* Messiah *with a symphony orchestra.*

A *joy for children of all ages,* The Nutcracker *is performed throughout the state by ballet companies of all sizes. The Colorado Ballet has been charming audiences with an annual Christmas production since 1960.*

Colorado Ballet

Denver Center Theatre

A *seasonal favorite is Charles Dickens'* A Christmas Carol, *performed by the Denver Center Theatre Company, the Rocky Mountain region's resident professional theatre ensemble. The actors are accompanied by members of the Colorado Symphony Orchestra and the Colorado Children's Chorale.*

Dickens Carolers

The Colorado Children's Chorale

The spirit of Christmas is always apparent in the voices of children singing. A very special Christmas present given to the people of Colorado is the gift of holiday music performed by the Colorado Children's Chorale.

We love candlelight Christmas Eve services and watching my sister's performances with the Colorado Children's Chorale.

— A.D., Denver

Norwest Bank Atrium

The Colorado Children's Chorale brings together two holiday favorites—music and children. More than 350 youths, age seven through thirteen, sing in the Chorale, known internationally for its talent, enthusiasm, and dedication.

Divided into five choirs that perform throughout the state during the course of the year, the Colorado Children's Chorale is in tremendous demand during the holidays. Their annual concert, "Christmas with the Children's Chorale," includes all the children and is a long-awaited event for many families throughout the region. The Chorale also appears with the Colorado Symphony Orchestra and Colorado Symphony Chorus in their annual Christmas concerts.

The children help light up the state by singing at the annual Norwest Tree Lighting Ceremony, taking place in the Norwest Bank Atrium in Denver, the Estes Park Community Performance at the Stanley Hotel, the Westminster Community Concert, and numerous other private and public celebrations.

State Captitol Building

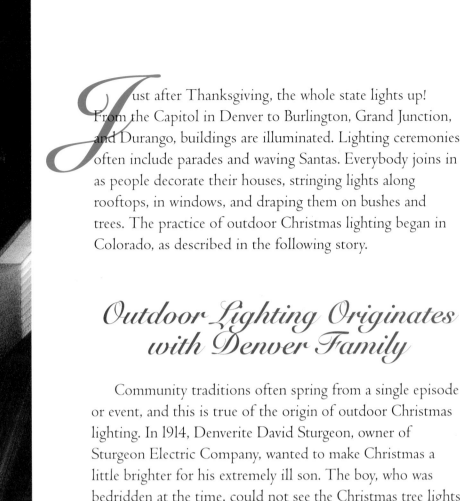

*J*ust after Thanksgiving, the whole state lights up! From the Capitol in Denver to Burlington, Grand Junction, and Durango, buildings are illuminated. Lighting ceremonies often include parades and waving Santas. Everybody joins in as people decorate their houses, stringing lights along rooftops, in windows, and draping them on bushes and trees. The practice of outdoor Christmas lighting began in Colorado, as described in the following story.

Outdoor Lighting Originates with Denver Family

Community traditions often spring from a single episode or event, and this is true of the origin of outdoor Christmas lighting. In 1914, Denverite David Sturgeon, owner of Sturgeon Electric Company, wanted to make Christmas a little brighter for his extremely ill son. The boy, who was bedridden at the time, could not see the Christmas tree lights that decorated the family's living room. So the elder Sturgeon took some ordinary light bulbs, dipped them in green and red paint, and strung them up on a pine tree outside young David's bedroom window.

Pleased with his success, the next year Sturgeon decorated several trees in his yard, and many of the neighbors joined in to light up their yards as well. The neighborhood soon became the talk of the town, and people came from all over the city to enjoy the spectacle.

In 1918, the late Frances Wayne, a reporter for *The Denver Post,* began a newspaper campaign, supported by the Denver Electrical League, that blossomed into a contest for the city's best outdoor lighting. Denverites marveled at these displays.

The idea soon spread to include civic buildings. John Malpiede, former city electrician, took on the task of creating an elaborate outdoor display for the City and County Building at Denver's Civic Center. Sturgeon Electric Company acted as a consultant and contributed extensively to the city's displays. To this day Sturgeon Electric continues to lend support in a variety of ways.

— Elaine Hughes
President, Keep the Lights Foundation

*O*n Christmas Eve, we like to drive through the streets of our neighborhood to see the Christmas lights! We play Christmas music on the radio, then go home and have a late dinner. On Christmas morning we get up late and have champagne and orange juice while opening gifts. Then we call our families in other states.

— L.S., Aurora

*W*hat makes the holidays special? The Parade of Lights!!!

— S.A.J., Lakewood

Georgetown Christmas Market

The holidays are extra special in Georgetown, a former mining town that boasts the oldest traditional Christmas market in the state. The Georgetown Christmas Market offers a glimpse of what life was like in the nineteenth century, as the residents of both Georgetown and Silver Plume invite visitors to become a part of their old-time holiday celebrations.

Under the sponsorship of Historic Georgetown, Inc., the local historical society, the people of Georgetown open their community and their hearts to all who want to enjoy a Colorado version of a small-town Victorian Christmas. During the first two weekends in December, the town prepares for the coming holidays with an authentic outdoor market. Visitors can buy handcrafted gifts, snack on chestnuts roasted over an open fire, or take a ride in a horse-drawn wagon. There are carolers dressed in Victorian garb, Santa Lucia processions, visits from Saint Nicholas, and community celebrations at the restored historic Hamill House and the luxurious Hotel de Paris.

Started in 1960, the Georgetown Christmas Market is based on celebrations typical of European mountain towns, especially the Swedish Julmarknad and the German Christmarket. As one wanders through the streets of Georgetown, the atmosphere evokes the feeling of what Christmas might have been like over a hundred years ago in the Rocky Mountain West. The Georgetown Christmas Market has become one of Colorado's favorite ways to proclaim the holiday season.

At Christmas
we love to watch
many versions of
Charles Dickens'
A Christmas Carol.

— J.H., Parker

An old-fashioned Christmas is celebrated in Georgetown.

The celebration of the feast of Santa Lucia is a cherished Swedish tradition. According to custom, the eldest daughter dresses in a simple white gown with a bright red sash. A crown of evergreens and lighted white candles carefully adorns her hair. It is her privilege to bake Lucia buns—or a favorite Colorado substitute of cinnamon rolls—which she serves to her family on December 13, the feast of Santa Lucia. The Eklund Family describes this special day as the beginning of their Christmas season.

What makes Christmas special for us? The Nutcracker ballet— even for cool teens — and watching White Christmas and It's a Wonderful Life on T.V. We also love the Festival of Trees.

— P.O., Westminster

Santa Lucia

We celebrate the feast of Santa Lucia, the Saint of Light, on December 13. We are given saffron bread and tea in bed at morning by our daughter. She arrives carrying the bread and wearing an all-white gown and a crown of candles, singing the song "Santa Lucia." Then she goes to school to share this with her classmates.

Our dream of a perfect Colorado Christmas is having our Swedish family visit our home and having the time filled with sledding and skiing on Christmas Day. We'd relax by the warmth of a crackling fire and nibble on leftovers from the previous night's smorgasbord. What Christmas brings to mind is family, sharing, laughing, warmth, love, skiing together, good food, and long memorable talks. It's the feelings and memories that continue.

— Pelle and Chris Eklund, Vail

Bent's Old Fort Hot Mulled Cider

4 2-inch cinnamon sticks
24 whole cloves
1 gallon apple cider
1 cup brown sugar
2 teaspoons ground allspice
1 teaspoon ground cinnamon

Tie cinnamon sticks and cloves in a cheesecloth, add to the rest of the ingredients, and heat, but do not boil. Simmer the cider mixture for at least 20 minutes. Ladle into large cups. If desired you may add grated nutmeg, a pat of butter, a dash of brandy—or all three. The aroma of this delicious brew will beckon guests to the cider bowl. Makes 16 to 20 servings.

Las Posadas

Those of Spanish heritage celebrate the Christmas season with traditional *las posadas*, colorful processions representing the journey of Mary and Joseph to Bethlehem. The procession is divided into two groups, one as travelers

and the other as innkeepers. Travelers carry candles and small statues of Mary and Joseph and approach the innkeepers looking for a place to stay, just as Mary and Joseph sought a room in the inns of Bethlehem. The innkeepers refuse the travelers a room. Finally, the travelers come to the room where the *nacimiento*, the nativity scene, has been arranged. It is here that the travelers and innkeepers meet for prayers followed by a Christmas party and feast.

A pinata, usually molded in the form of an animal, is filled with small gifts and treats. It is hung high, and the children take turns batting at it with a stick to try to break it open. When the pinata finally bursts, the gifts and treats fall to the floor and the children scramble to share in the bounty.

aring for community members is a long-standing Colorado tradition. In the late 1800s Denver was the birthplace of the world's largest voluntary human services movement—United Way—which was initially known as the Charity Organization Society of Denver.

The spirit of helping and giving continues today. Starting in November, Christmas bazaars sponsored by non-profit and community organizations provide festive venues for holiday shopping. Collected canned goods and money contributions assure that those less fortunate will be able to celebrate the Christmas season. Pageants, parties, and special events also help raise money for those in need.

Molly Brown, famous for courageously surviving the sinking of the "unsinkable" Titanic in 1912, made sure that children in Denver and Leadville orphanages had hats, scarves, and gloves to protect them from the cold Colorado winters every year.

❋   ❋   ❋

At *Cleveholm Manor* in Redstone, coal and steel baron John Cleveland Osgood and his wife, Alma, are remembered for their generosity. In the early 1900s, Alma became known as Lady Bountiful; she would find out what each child in town wanted for Christmas, then locate and purchase those gifts in shops from Denver to New York.

❋   ❋   ❋

Operation Christmas is a special event sponsored by the *USAF Academy* cadets. Each year the Cadet Wing hosts a Christmas party for underprivileged children in Colorado Springs. Funded solely by voluntary donations from cadets, Operation Christmas provides a toy for each child.

❋   ❋   ❋

Old Fashioned Christmas in Kiowa, sponsored by the Volunteer Fire Department, invites everyone in the community to bring a dish to share. This gathering began as a way to thank the families in the area for the sacrifices they make during the year when emergency personnel are called away from home. Now it welcomes all, especially newcomers.

L'Esprit de Noel Home Tour is sponsored by the Central City Opera House Association Guild. Private homes, decorated by top floral designers, are opened for tours on the first weekend in December.

❋   ❋   ❋

Coloradans living near Burlington are treated to a *Carousel Christmas.* Normally open from Memorial Day to Labor Day, the Kit Carson County Carousel is especially festive on the first Sunday in December. The hand-carved carousel animals are decorated with red and silver bows. The entertainment offered during this community appreciation celebration includes free rides, Christmas music playing on the magnificent Wurlitzer, hot cider, and a visit from Father Christmas.

❋   ❋   ❋

The *ArtReach Festival of Trees* in Denver fuses the holiday spirit with creativity and generosity. The magic of a hundred Christmas trees, all decorated differently, is just the beginning. Funds produced from this event provide arts programs and performances to people who might not otherwise experience the rich culture available in Colorado.

When I am not able to be with my family on Christmas, I like to spend my day at the Samaritan House, giving of my time.

— J.D., Denver

$\mathcal{C}$olorado's historic hotels and homes host countless events, performances, parties, dinners, and teas to ring in the Christmas season with a flurry of Victorian elegance.

The Broadmoor

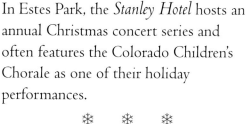

In Estes Park, the *Stanley Hotel* hosts an annual Christmas concert series and often features the Colorado Children's Chorale as one of their holiday performances.

❆　❆　❆

Central City's *Wintershire* open houses have been held since the 1930s and include public tours through the historic Teller House as well as through Victorian homes, churches, and museums. The open houses are held each year on the three days after Thanksgiving.

❆　❆　❆

The two-story adobe *Baca House* in Trinidad, lit by kerosene lamps inside and luminarias outside, highlights Hispanic Christmas traditions of the 1870s.

❆　❆　❆

$\mathcal{W}$e celebrate by having brunch at the Broadmoor, walking around the lake and taking our Christmas family picture.

— N.S.G., Littleton

The Broadmoor in Colorado Springs celebrates "A Colorado Christmas at the Broadmoor" with lavish feasts, musical entertainment, ice skating extravaganzas performed by the Broadmoor Skating Club, and performances by the Colorado Springs Symphony Orchestra. The Broadmoor dresses for the holidays by stringing more than 200,000 white lights on the hotel and grounds.

❆　❆　❆

The Brown Palace

The Brown Palace hotel in downtown Denver is a distinguished Colorado landmark. It has operated continuously since 1892 and has hosted dignitaries from all over the world. Its festive Christmas lights and decor make it a favorite choice for holiday parties, teas, and brunches.

In Pueblo, the *Rosemount Victorian House Museum* gives meaning to its motto, "Where the elegant East met the rugged West!" Furnished with many original period pieces, this 37-room mansion is festively decorated for the holidays.

The Rosemount Victorian House Museum

The Rosemount Victorian House Museum

The *Molly Brown House Museum* on Denver's Capitol Hill features Victorian Christmas decorations and Candlelight Tours during the holiday season. In addition, formal Victorian dinner parties and teas may be arranged for groups wishing to celebrate in the lavish style of Molly Brown.

✽   ✽   ✽

Owned and operated by a third-generation pioneer family, the *Castle Marne* in Denver invites guests to holiday teas and to assist in decorating during the weeks before Christmas. Other inns and bed and breakfasts around the state follow similar customs.

✽   ✽   ✽

Country Christmas at Cross Orchards Historic Site in Grand Junction celebrates with carols and horse-drawn hay wagon rides—traditional holiday activities on a turn-of-the-century farm.

✽   ✽   ✽

Four Mile Historic Park, a stage stop four miles from Denver on the Cherokee Trail, hosts an 1880s holiday open house where visitors talk with Santa, ride in a stagecoach, and enjoy Christmas music and storytelling. Early settlers celebrated with foods from the plains, most likely wild fowl, venison, or buffalo, as well as an English plum pudding, possibly made with pumpkin.

On the night after Thanksgiving, the streets of Redstone are lined with candeleria and a bonfire roars at the *Redstone Inn* for the town's Grand Illumination. To usher in the Christmas season, children sing at Cleveholm Manor and sleighs transport guests around this quaint village, located in the Crystal River Valley.

The Redstone Inn

✽   ✽   ✽

Aspen silver baron Jerome B. Wheeler built a stately brick Queen Anne Victorian home in 1888. It now houses the *Wheeler-Stallard House Museum,* reflecting the grandeur of Aspen at Christmas. The museum hosts carols sung by the Aspen Children's Choir, Christmas stories, and visits with Santa.

✽   ✽   ✽

Not all historic places were hotels or private homes. *The Ouray County Museum,* built in 1887 as St. Joseph's Hospital and run by the Sisters of Mercy, is decorated in a Victorian manner with antique dolls and toys. The furnishings include an ornately carved piano from Ouray's notorious Gold Belt Theatre—with a bullet hole near middle C!

The Ouray County Museum

A Christmas Tradition of Ouray County

As frost touches the area and leaves start to fall, the thoughts and efforts of Ouray's Benevolent and Protective Order of Elks, along with those of its Ladies Auxiliary, are directed towards planning the annual Christmas Program.

In 1928, the Elks offered to help Santa make sure that each child, house-bound person, and senior citizen in Ouray County received a sack of Christmas cheer from Santa Claus on Christmas Eve. Today, this program requires a monumental effort on the part of all those involved.

Serious planning starts in late September when the Santa suits are cleaned and inspected, candy and nuts are ordered, and the committee chairman starts a campaign to recruit drivers for the vehicles and people to fill the Santa suits.

The week prior to Christmas Eve is devoted to final preparations. The Ladies Auxiliary meets in Ouray and Ridgway to produce nearly 1,200 popcorn balls. Members of the lodge and the auxiliary meet at the Elks Home to complete the sacking. Tables are set up in an assembly line and everyone pitches in to fill, staple, and pack the sacks. Half of them are taken to Ridgway and half are kept in Ouray. Anyone with a special request may contact the Elks Home in advance.

On Christmas Eve, teams of Santas and drivers meet at designated locations. They cover the entire county, using four-wheel-drive vehicles over the area's 540 square miles, much of it vertical. The drivers, affectionately called "Rudolphs," concentrate on navigating the snow-packed roads so the Santas can focus on the important work of distributing sacks. Residents are requested to have their porch lights turned on to ensure that a Santa will visit.

Darkness comes early at this time of year, and the Santas are on their way by 5:30 p.m., completing the visits before bedtime for the little ones. If all goes well, rounds are finished by 9:00 p.m. and the Santas and their helpers can relax until next year.

— Ouray Lodge No. 492, B.P.O.E

Grinch Turned Santa

Throughout the years, I have become somewhat of a grinch when it comes to Christmas. Some years ago, one of the Santas was called out of town on an emergency. I was more or less railroaded into filling the vacancy with the Ouray County Elks. It took several well-placed pillows to convert me into the jolly fat man, and after a crash course in learning how to properly "Ho, Ho, Ho!", I was ready.

As I left the Elks with my bagful of goodies, I was praying I could make it through the night without strangling one of the little monsters. It took visits to a couple of houses before I got into the groove of things and the joy of Christmas began to prevail.

At one house, the little boy who lived there could not have candy. However, his parents had previously left a package at the Elks to be delivered by Santa. The little boy was elated that Santa knew of his problem and had brought him a toy instead of candy.

Another house had two huge black dogs that looked the size of Angus bulls. Their idea of fun was to see how many laps old Santa could make around the house before they exposed his backside to the elements. After a lap and a half, the owner finally opened the door and in flew Santa. No time for the old chimney routine.

At yet another house, two cute little girls opened the front door when Santa arrived. By checking my list ahead of time, I knew the children by name and age. But this particular house was missing one child. I asked the little girls where their brother was, and they informed me that he was in the bathtub and had the chicken pox. As I was giving the little girls their treats, I heard a splish splash. Out of the bathroom came the little boy, overjoyed at the sight of Santa. I mean this kid was buck naked. The only thing he had on was the chicken pox. Up on my lap he leaped and a better hug have I yet to receive.

The Christmas treats are purchased by the Elks from their charity fund, money raised through contributions to the Christmas program as well as the annual Charity Ball and annual horseback Ride for Charity. All Santas, Rudolphs, and vehicles are furnished by Elks members.

If you have friends in Ouray County and really want something different to do Christmas Eve, go visit them and watch the Ouray Elks at work. It will be an experience you will never forget. You'll be quick to realize that brotherly love and the Christmas spirit really do exist.

— A Former Grinch

We have community-wide caroling. There is a big tree lit on the hill in town and a lighted star on the mountainside.

— S.L., Ouray

*C*hristmas carols learned during childhood continue to ring in our hearts, especially during community celebrations. Caroling parties bring people together to sing their favorite songs and socialize over potluck feasts.

In *Grand Lake*, Colorado's oldest resort, caroling is a cherished Christmas tradition. It is not unusual to have more than 200 people start at the Chapel in the Pines and sing carols while strolling the snow-packed main street, stopping at any open establishment along the way. The carolers finish at the other end of town, where they are invited into St. Anne's Church for refreshments. The Grand Lake caroling party is usually held on the last Sunday before Christmas Eve and is open to anyone who would like to join in.

In the first Saturday in December, *Limon's* residents and visitors celebrate with caroling, roasted chestnuts, a craft market, a Tree Walk, and Santa's arrival.

❄   ❄   ❄

A Chocolate Tasting Extravaganza takes place in *Creede* in late November. Carolers entertain shoppers as they sample chocolate in every size, color, and description.

❄   ❄   ❄

Telluride's Noel Night is held during the first week of December. Store owners stay open late into the night, with many serving snacks and drinks, such as wassail, mulled wine, and hot chocolate for the kids. Serenaded by carolers, locals wander up and down the streets visiting with neighbors and friends as they search for the perfect gift.

❄   ❄   ❄

One of *Denver's* largest Christmas bazaars is sponsored by the Junior League. The Annual Holiday Mart features items and foods from all over the world. It is a wonderful place to hear the many sounds of the season as performed by numerous church choirs, bell choirs, and singing groups.

❄   ❄   ❄

The tree lighting and caroling party in *Ridgway* is right after Thanksgiving. Gathering around a large bonfire, members of the community sing in the season. Refreshments are served and Santa shows up in a horse-drawn sleigh to join in the festivities. The week before Christmas, a community choir presents a "Special Music of Christmas" program at a local church.

In Aspen, as in many towns throughout the state, church members meet for a meal before venturing out in the cold to go caroling. This menu for a Buffalo Chili Supper is sure to warm your caroling party.

Buffalo Chili Supper

Buffalo Chile Rojo Con Carne

Corn Spoon Bread

Assorted Christmas Cookies

Hot Chocolate with Peppermint Candy Canes

Bent's Old Fort Hot Mulled Cider*

* Check Recipe Index for listing.

Buffalo Chile Rojo Con Carne

1 pound ground buffalo meat
2 tablespoons canola oil
5 tablespoons chili powder
¾ cup onion, chopped
½ tablespoon garlic, chopped
1¼ cups tomatoes, diced
1 tablespoon vinegar
1 teaspoon ground coriander

⅛ teaspoon ground cloves
1 teaspoon cumin
1 tablespoon oregano
2 teaspoons brown sugar
3 cups beef consomme
12 ounces red kidney beans, drained
12 ounces pinto beans, drained

In a deep pot, brown buffalo meat in oil. Add onions and cook until tender. Combine all ingredients in pot and simmer for 2 hours. Serves 6 to 8 people.

— Dave LaGant and Will McFarlane
Denver Buffalo Company

Playing Christmas music, caroling, and delivering cookies to friends and neighbors make our Christmas special.

— H.W., Thornton

Corn Spoon Bread

This cornbread recipe goes well with chili or soups.

2 eggs, slightly beaten
1 8-ounce package Jiffy Corn Muffin Mix
1 8-ounce can cream-style corn
1 8-ounce can whole kernel corn, drained

1 cup sour cream
½ cup butter, melted
1 cup swiss cheese, shredded

Mix together all ingredients except cheese. Place the batter in an 8x8-inch pan. Bake at 350 degrees for 35 minutes. Sprinkle with cheese and bake for 10 to 15 minutes more. Serves 9.

— Jan Kiefer

As in many regions of the country, Christmas cards are a time-honored tradition in Colorado. One town has a special season's greetings stamp, and another displays card scenes and sayings in mural form. Card programs sometimes raise funds for a particular purpose, such as a charity or to support the town's lighting traditions.

The following descriptions represent a few of the interesting Christmas card customs found around the state.

Volunteers donate a little time each day to stamp Christmas greetings on cards sent to *Holly*, Colorado's Christmas City, for remailing. Cards should reach Holly about a week before Christmas to insure remailing in time for Christmas delivery.

The Holly Christmas mark adds a bit of Colorado to your Christmas cards. To have yours stamped and remailed, send them with the proper postage in a larger envelope to:

Holly Christmas Remailing
c/o Holly Commercial Club
P.O. Box 114
Holly, CO 81047

An *Estes Park* tradition features Santa's Christmas Card Studio. These hand-painted scenes by artist Buel Porter are free-standing, larger-than-life-size wooden murals displayed around town during the Christmas season.

❄   ❄   ❄

Durango raises funds to light and decorate its streets by selling the Durango Christmas card. "Winter Dream," an oil painting of the Durango & Silverton Narrow Gauge Railroad, has been reproduced on the card's cover. Portrayed by artist Roland E. Rustad, the painting was lovingly donated by his wife, Pat.

❄   ❄   ❄

Keep the Lights Foundation publishes a Christmas card featuring the lighting of Denver's City and County Building, a 60-year-old tradition. Money raised from the card helps to support the yearly display.

❄   ❄   ❄

Christmas card programs across the state raise funds for a variety of good causes. *The Children's Hospital* in Denver sells Christmas cards designed by young patients; the proceeds assist the hospital in treating pediatric cancer patients.

A long-standing Colorado tradition lights up the state from Thanksgiving through the end of the National Western in mid-January. Nearly every town and resort has a tree lighting ceremony and a parade of lights that heralds the Christmas season. A sampling of these events is listed here.

Vail Valley's Festival of Lights is a magical holiday event geared towards families. Encompassing Avon, Beaver Creek, and Vail, each town puts on activities that include carolers, town criers, Santa and his elves, and window decorations.

❋　❋　❋

Glenwood Springs hosts a Luminaria Lighting Celebration and Candlelight Holiday Walk that features old-fashioned luminarias, caroling, and evening shopping.

❋　❋　❋

Idaho Springs' Christmas Tree Lighting includes caroling, the lighting of the municipal tree, roasted chestnuts, and hot cider. Shops stay open late throughout downtown.

❋　❋　❋

In mid-December, the *Burlington* Parade of Lights delights spectators with floats, antique cars, and horse-drawn buggies through the main street of town. The parade ends in Old Town, where refreshments are served.

❋　❋　❋

Castle Rock's annual Star Lighting Ceremony brings the whole community together just before Thanksgiving.

16th St. Mall, Denver

Blossoms of Light, a tradition at *Denver Botanic Gardens*, glows with professionally designed light displays through the month of December. Wander among intricately woven vignettes of giant flowers, spiral trees, oak twig reindeer, and a decorative Santa Claus. The Botanic Gardens also hosts holiday concerts and Teddy Bear teas.

❋　❋　❋

Estes Park hosts a Come Catch the Glow Christmas Parade, featuring floats strung with lights. Activities begin with the town's famous wildlife characters—people dressed as elk, bighorn sheep, deer, and foxes—strolling the downtown area visiting with children of all ages.

❋　❋　❋

The Santa Claus Parade in *Elizabeth* brings jolly old Saint Nick to town. After the parade, which is held on the Saturday before Christmas, there is caroling, a community dinner, and pictures with Santa.

❋　❋　❋

Gunnison's 60-year-old tradition includes an annual parade to light the giant Christmas tree in the center of town.

Denver City and County Building

The world's largest Christmas lighting display takes place in Denver from December 1st until after the National Western in January. Preceded by the News 4 Parade of Lights, more than 40,000 colored floodlights and bulbs are illuminated to decorate the City and County Building. For the lighting ceremony, Christmas carols are played in the ten-chime tower while thousands of people gather in front of the building and in nearby Civic Center Park to witness this spectacular display of lights.

The Keep the Lights Foundation raises money for the lighting of the City and County Building, a spectacular gift to Denver and the state of Colorado.

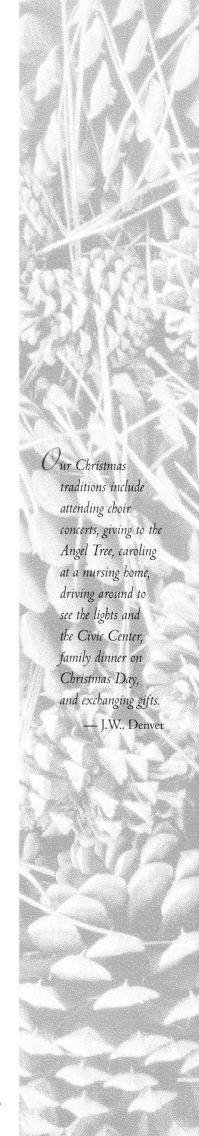

Our Christmas traditions include attending choir concerts, giving to the Angel Tree, caroling at a nursing home, driving around to see the lights and the Civic Center, family dinner on Christmas Day, and exchanging gifts.
— J.W., Denver

Castle Creek, near Aspen

Colorado Outdoors

You can find a picture-perfect Christmas setting right here in Colorado. It's the champagne snow, the sunny days, and the quiet serenity of star-filled nights! Mining brought adventurers to the state during the 1800s; today it's the snow and scenery that keeps us here and draws millions of visitors from around the world. ❄ Colorado boasts an average of 300 sunny days a year, but the nights—clear and crisp and sparkling—are what make winter special. It's not unusual to go to sleep with the snow just starting to fall and wake up to a bright powder day. That's the ultimate Colorado Christmas experience! Downhill skiers race to be first in the lift line, and cross-country skiers fill their backpacks with picnic lunches and head for the high country. ❄ As Coloradans we spend a great deal of time out-of-doors, and the holiday season is no exception. With friends and family we hike into the forest to cut Christmas trees, attend yule log festivals, and ride Santa trains with our children. And what's more festive than being snuggled under a blanket in a horse-drawn sleigh decorated with greenery, bows, and bells? ❄ To spend Christmas in Colorado, amid the spectacular scenery of the Rocky Mountains, is to truly feel the wonder and magic of the season.

We always start the holiday season by cutting our own tree in the mountains not too far from town. The whole family joins in the search for the perfect tree. One year our young son, Stefan, asked if I thought the tree would be sad because we were going to kill it. He explained that the Indians always said a prayer to the spirit of the deer before slaying it, seeking forgiveness and thanking it for providing food. He paused, closed his eyes briefly, and then happily told us it was all right to go ahead with the saw. Somehow, the decorated Christmas tree really did seem prettier than usual that year.

—The K.M. Family, Denver

Tree shapes, Sawatch Range

O Christmas Tree!

Christmas trees bring the sights and scents of the forest into our homes. Colorado is a state of living Christmas trees—all year long. Douglas fir, ponderosa pine, and our state tree— the blue spruce—are all native to Colorado. The adventure of cutting your own Christmas tree is a Rocky Mountain tradition too good to miss.

Permits for cutting trees are available from the National Forest Service and the Colorado State Forest Service. Designated tree-cutting areas help to manage our renewable natural resources. You may also visit a tree farm or harvest a tree from your own property. Permits can usually be obtained during the first two weekends after Thanksgiving.

Experienced Christmas tree hunters suggest that you be prepared for moderately deep snow, dress warmly in layers, and bring a strong rope to tie the tree to the car. Snowshoes and cross-country skis can be helpful, as are snowmobiles. Looking for just the right tree is half the fun. When you find it, use either an axe or hand saw— no chain saws. The joyful experience of cutting your own Christmas tree brings the outdoors inside during the holiday season!

Palmer Lake's Yule Log Festivities

The yule log ceremony is an old-world custom that has been revived in the West. The oldest yule log tradition in Colorado takes place in Palmer Lake. It all began in 1933, when a minister at the Little Log Church wrote to the Lake Placid Yule Log Committee in New York requesting a splinter of their log.

The official yule log is about eight feet long, notched in the middle, and identified with a red bow. The event takes place in early afternoon after a logger has hidden the yule log. Two trumpeters, arriving in town especially for the ceremony, enter town hall followed by the logger. After the horns are sounded, red and green capes are passed out to all participants, who are then led to the search area.

Whoever finds the log rides it as it's dragged back to town and then drinks the first cup of wassail. Afterwards, the lucky person chops the log in half with an axe. One half of the log is saved as kindling for next year's yule log. The other half is burned with the log saved from the previous year.

The hunt itself only takes about 45 minutes. For those not wanting to brave the cold, a program of carols and other entertainment is held in town hall. Each participant and visitor gets a small yule log memento to wear, prepared by members of the community during an early December potluck supper. The keepsakes—small, notched branches—are stamped with the date and tied with red and green ribbons.

The Yule Log

During the Middle Ages, people celebrated Christmas with feasting, drinking wassail, and bringing in the yule log. Gradually the ideas of peace and good will were incorporated, feuds were ended and quarreling forbidden during Yuletide, which lasted from Christmas to Twelfth Night. Yule log ceremonies are held throughout Colorado, including the towns of Silverton, Beulah, Frisco, and Palmer Lake.

*A*fter a snowstorm, when the sun shines brightly, the whole world seems to sparkle like diamonds. This gift of nature provides an ideal environment for outdoor activities, including sledding, skiing, skating, snowmobiling—and even eating snow ice cream.

Sledding

A snowy slope and a couple of kids—of any age—can make for an eventful day outdoors. And if you don't have a sled, a little imagination works wonders. You can use a saucer, an inner tube, a plastic bag, or even a piece of cardboard. A few of these makeshift sleds may not turn too well, but then rolling in the snow is half the fun!

Skiing

Colorado is known for its downhill skiing. Light, dry snow makes for skiing that is unequalled elsewhere, whether it be groomed intermediate slopes, bone-jarring bump runs, or knee-deep powder tracks through the trees. Colorado resorts are known throughout the world—and for good reason.

Snow Sculptures

Snow Sculpture contests in Breckenridge allow each team to work with a 10x10x12-foot chunk of snow weighing 22 tons. The snow art is constructed over several days by groups from all over the world. Sculptures depict anything and everything, from dragons and castles to cowboy boots to skiers. Young, would-be sculptors get their start by practicing on snow forts.

Snow Ice Cream

1 large bowl of fresh snow
1½ to 2 cups of half-and-half or heavy cream
2 tablespoons vanilla extract
1¼ cups powdered sugar, sifted

Pour cream and vanilla over snow. Gradually add powdered sugar until well blended. Be careful not to let it melt. Add more snow if ice cream is too thin or more sugar if not sweet enough. Eat immediately.

Snowmobiling

Snowmobiling tours from the T-Lazy-7 Ranch in Aspen take guests up to the scenic Maroon Bells, where hot refreshments are served by the lake. Between Christmas and the New Year, folks in Lake City take advantage of the excellent snowmobiling, cross-country skiing, and ice fishing around beautiful Lake San Cristobal. Snowmobiles can be rented just about anywhere, but the snowmobile capitol is Grand Lake, where groomed trails lead riders into Rocky Mountain National Park.

Broomball

Children of all ages have a great time playing broomball. Using a broom to hit a large ball around the ice rink, this sport often replaces ice hockey for afternoon outdoor fun.

Skating

Ice skating rinks come in all shapes and sizes. They can be homemade (using landscape logs to form a pond), professional Olympic-size rinks, or a body of water, like Keystone Lake. Ouray's skating rink and warming hut, located near Box Canyon Falls, is open days and evenings. At Jorgensen Park in Gunnison, outdoor skating ponds are open from December through February. Evergreen Lake, accessible to the metro-Denver area, has been a popular spot for generations of ice skating enthusiasts.

We celebrate Christmas by being together...and by taking a moonlight snowmobile ride.

— Anonymous, Craig

Our holiday wish is to have an old-fashioned Christmas with our kids spending the time in the mountains, skiing, tubing, tobogganing, and skating.

— H.W., Thornton

Cross-country skiers enjoy the snow throughout the state, whether it be in city parks, on golf courses, in national forests, at ski areas, or on backcountry touring trails. At the Nordic Center in Frisco, for example, groomed, set tracks draw skiers to the shores of Lake Dillon. Outdoor activities such as nordic skiing burn calories quickly and produce hearty appetites. This portable snow picnic satisfies even the hungriest outdoor enthusiasts.

Snow Picnic

Sam Arnold's
Buffalo Stew in Red Wine*
Individual Sheepherder Loaves
Marinated Winter Vegetables
Bent's Old Fort Hot Spiced Cider*
Red Pears
Cranberry Date Bars*

* Check Recipe Index for listings.

Snowstorm in the Gunnison National Forest

Sam Arnold's Buffalo Stew in Red Wine

This stew is delicious and better than the first kiss!

Herb bouquet tied in cheesecloth:
6 parsley stems
1 teaspoon thyme
2-3 whole garlic cloves
3 cloves
1 bay leaf
4 allspice berries
6 peppercorns

3 pounds trimmed buffalo round,
  cut into 2-inch chunks
1 cup tomatoes, chopped
2 tablespoons cornstarch
1 tablespoon butter
2 tablespoons white vermouth
1 teaspoon oil
5 to 6 white cooked turnips,
  cut in large chunks
salt to taste
1 cup each sauteed carrots,
  onions, and celery, sliced
4 to 5 cooked carrots, cut in lengths
6 cooked potatoes, cut in large ovals
3 to 4 cups red wine or
  2 cups beef stock

Brown meat on all sides in butter and oil. Season with salt and arrange in a casserole dish with the sauteed vegetables. Cover with red wine or beef stock. Add the herb bouquet to the casserole, then add tomatoes. Cover the casserole and simmer until tender, about 2½ hours. Drain the sauce and save. Return the meat to the casserole dish. De-grease the sauce and thicken with cornstarch mixed with white vermouth. Simmer the sauce about 2 minutes and pour over the meat. Fold in the cooked vegetables. Simmer for 4 to 5 minutes, basting the meat. Serves 12.

— Sam Arnold,
The Fort Restaurant

91

*Torchlight parade
and fireworks, Aspen*

Our favorite tradition is picking out and cutting down our tree from the hill behind our cabin. It's always a funny, odd-looking tree that needs to be thinned from the forest. When its decorated it's the most beautiful Christmas tree!

— B.B., Boulder

C Lazy U Ranch

Dogsled trips through wilderness areas offer an exciting way to enjoy mountain scenery in winter. Some sled dogs, commonly referred to as Huskies, are hybrids of three original sled dog breeds—Malamute, Eskimo, and Siberian.

❄   ❄   ❄

Torchlight parades brighten the Christmas season with colorful nighttime displays at ski areas throughout the state. Carrying lighted flares, experienced skiers snake down the mountain in perfect formation with fireworks illuminating the slopes—a combination of Christmas, Fourth of July, and Mardi Gras.

Winding River Resort

The perfect Colorado Christmas would be a two-week retreat to a lodge outside Steamboat Springs with all the families of our brothers and sisters gathering to cross-country ski, snowshoe, and go on sleigh rides.

— The K.B. Family, Parker

Our ideal Colorado Christmas would be to stay in a wonderful, cozy mountain lodge and celebrate with a traditional Christmas dinner. We would ski, hike, sit around the fire and drink hot chocolate with the entire family.

— S.C., Colorado Springs

Georgetown

Dashing Through the Snow... Colorado Style!

Through snow-hushed forests and fields, the sounds of people singing and bells jingling fill the air as a team of draft horses pulls a sleigh of joyous passengers.

Sleigh rides are a favorite holiday tradition in Colorado. In mountain towns and ski areas, horse-drawn sleighs prove a relaxing diversion from more rigorous winter activities. What was once a major form of family transportation now brings families and friends together for a uniquely Colorado outdoor experience.

At the Winding River Resort in Grand Lake, a matched set of sorrel-colored Belgians named Amy and Liz tow an antique sleigh through a winter wonderland. The 125-year-old sled, originally a trolley from Chicago, has a tasseled roof and open sides so passengers can fully enjoy the scenery of nearby Rocky Mountain National Park. The driver's colorful stories add an extra touch that makes this ride classic Colorado.

Old-fashioned sleigh rides at the C Lazy U Ranch are available on winter afternoons courtesy of Levi and Strauss, two beautiful Belgian draft horses each weighing more than 2,000 pounds. If guests wish to take part in the day-to-day activities of a working ranch, they can help feed the herd of 160 horses that winters in the pasture.

At Keystone Ranch, a young cowboy—complete with Stetson, duster, weather-worn boots, a broad grin, and a guitar—provides entertainment for the evening. The ride follows a trail through Arapaho National Forest to the old homestead place, with a stop for dinner at the Reynolds Cabin, a bunkhouse built in the 1920s.

Regardless of the length of the trip, a sleigh ride through the Colorado landscape is sure to make your spirits bright.

Granby

We'd like to spend Christmas in Steamboat Springs, riding in a horse-drawn sleigh and sipping champagne. Just being together as a couple.

— J.B.,
Highlands Ranch

I'd like to spend Christmas in a cabin with a big fireplace!

— R.R., Pueblo

Our wish for a perfect Colorado Christmas is to have all my relatives flown in from out-of-state to a cabin in the mountains. There would be a big hill to go sledding and a roaring fire in the fireplace!

— The H. Family,
Westminster

On Christmas Eve we stay up late and open presents. On Christmas Day we ski as a family and then eat a big dinner.

— J.R.,
Crested Butte

We have a snow hill up the street and love to go sledding.

— The R.C. Family,
Broomfield

Covered Bridge, Vail

Colorado offers some of the world's best snow skiing, the result of a dry climate and mountainous terrain. Throughout winter, downhill ski resorts and nordic areas provide skiers with thousands of vertical feet and miles of groomed trails. Some locations, such as Vail and Steamboat Springs, even have bobsled runs.

Whatever your sport of choice, be it "shredding" the mountain on a snowboard or leisurely cruising down blue runs, the time comes when the lifts close and the sun sinks behind the mountain. After the day's strenuous activities, it's time to unbuckle your boots and relax.

This is when friends gather to relive the events of the day, from that spectacular mogul run to the faceplant worthy of movie stuntmen. Après ski activities are usually casual affairs—meeting for a beer or cafe latte, gathering around a fondue pot, or soaking in a hot tub. The natural mineral pools at Glenwood Springs are perfect for après ski relaxation.

Snow angels inhabit Colorado!

The best ones appear when there is about eight inches of snow on the ground. To make a snow angel, you simply fall backwards into a pile of new-fallen snow. Then you flap your arms up and down and your legs open and closed. When you stand up, it will look as if an angel has left an imprint in the snow.

One of our Christmas traditions is to string popcorn and cranberries on the Christmas tree. We make extra strands to decorate the trees and bushes outside, which feeds the sparrows and squirrels.

— The J.O.K. Family, Aurora

We always begin our holiday season at the Parker County Christmas Parade.

— The K.B. Family, Parker

Reindeer

Christmastime is when children dream of Santa and his sleigh of eight tiny reindeer. While the animals are not common in the United States outside of Alaska, the largest herd in the lower 48 states is found in Colorado at the Flying Deer Ranch near Snowmass. Some of these reindeer pull sleighs in Denver's Parade of Lights. One wonders if reindeer really do head to the North Pole if given the chance.

My perfect Christmas? Lounging on a beach in Maui!

— C.D., Telluride

Colorado Cowboy Cookout

Colorado traditionally ends the holiday season with the National Western Stock Show. You can celebrate this annual event with a Cowboy Cookout featuring regional foods.

Colorado Lamb on a Spit
Pan Fried Trout*
Sage Camp Biscuits
Potato and Asparagus Skillet*
Apple Cinnamon Nut Cobbler*

* Check Recipe Index for listing.

Colorado lamb on a spit

*National Western
Stock Show & Rodeo*

Pan Fried Trout

Ice-fishing, a favorite Colorado winter sport, provides fabulous fresh trout for this recipe.

12 8- to 10-ounce trout, boneless
salt, pepper and garlic powder
4 cups flour

2 cups olive oil
2 lemons

Season trout with salt, pepper, and garlic powder. Dredge trout in flour. Heat olive oil in iron skillet and fry trout until golden brown on both sides. Check for doneness by inserting a knife into the dorsal fin; fish will flake when done. Place trout on platter and squeeze lemon juice over it before serving. Serves 12.

Potato and Asparagus Skillet

This colorful dish could be a meal by itself! — [Ed.]

½ pound bacon, diced
6 medium red potatoes,
    diced into ½-inch cubes
2 pounds of asparagus,
    cut into 1-inch pieces

2 red peppers, sliced thin
1 bunch green onions, diced
2 teaspoons salt
1 tablespoon black pepper
1 tablespoon rosemary

Cook bacon in skillet until almost crisp. Add potatoes and cook until tender. Add remaining ingredients and cook another three minutes. Serves 10 to 12.

Apple Cinnamon Nut Cobbler

This recipe was developed to feed the crew of a cattle round-up. It makes a lot, but the recipe can be reduced to suit your needs.

4 7-ounce Martha White Apple
    Cinnamon muffin mixes
2 cups milk
2 sticks butter

6 apples, sliced
1 pound brown sugar
8 ounces walnuts

Preheat dutch oven in campfire. Combine muffin mix and milk. Slice apples. Remove dutch oven from fire and melt butter in pan. Layer apples, brown sugar, and walnuts. Pour muffin mix on top. Cover and place dutch oven back into fire and cover with coals. Bake 15 minutes, then remove and serve. If not cooked enough, place back in fire for a few minutes. Feeds 12 hungry cowboys.

The Cowboy Cookout and recipes were developed by Jim Schlarbaum, Director of Operations for Epicurean Catering in Denver, and Tim Luksa, Epicurean's Executive Chef. Both are avid sportsmen and acclaimed Colorado chefs.

We like to go to Winter Park, Steamboat, or Breckenridge for the holidays!

— S.L.D.,
Northglenn

My Christmas wish is to have all of my children and their families coming to spend the holidays in the Colorado mountains.

— L.W.,
Grand Junction

Durango & Silverton Narrow Gauge Railroad

Rio Grande Denver Ski Train

Santa's Winter Trains

In Colorado, Santa Claus has been known to use a ski lift, a snowmobile, skis, and even trains to make pre-Christmas visits. In Georgetown, Santa gives his reindeer a chance to graze while he rides the Santa's Express Train and listens to the wishes of young passengers.

For Lamar's Enchanted Forest, real pine trees come alive with the magic of Christmas. There is entertainment, decorated trees, visits to Santa's cabin, and miniature train rides for the children.

Since 1940, Coloradans and visitors have enjoyed the experience of riding the Rio Grande Ski Train. On weekend mornings during the ski season, the train makes a two-hour trip from historic Union Station in Denver to the base of Winter Park Resort. At the end of the day it makes the return trip with a trainload of tired skiers.

From Thanksgiving through December 31, excluding Christmas Eve and Christmas Day, the Durango & Silverton Narrow Gauge Railroad's Winter Holidays train chugs through mountainous snowscapes between Durango and Cascade Canyon. Originally built to transport gold and silver from the mines to the mills, this historic, coal-fired train now takes passengers on scenic sightseeing tours.

Next year we would like to rent a large cabin in Glenwood Springs, ride Amtrak up from Denver, and bring along family and friends to just enjoy.

— D.F., Aurora

Georgetown
Loop
Railroad

Silent Night

Silent night, Holy night!

All is calm, All is bright.
'Round yon Virgin Mother and Child
Holy Infant so tender and mild
Sleep in heavenly peace,
Sleep in heavenly peace!

Silent night, Holy night!
Shepherds quake at the sight!
Glories stream from heaven afar,
Heavenly hosts sing Alleluia,
Christ, the Savior, is born!
Christ, the Savior, is born!

Silent night, Holy night!
Son of God, love's pure light
Radiant beams from Thy holy face,
With the dawn of Redeeming grace,
Jesus, Lord at Thy birth,
Jesus, Lord at Thy birth.

Star Peak, Elk Mountains

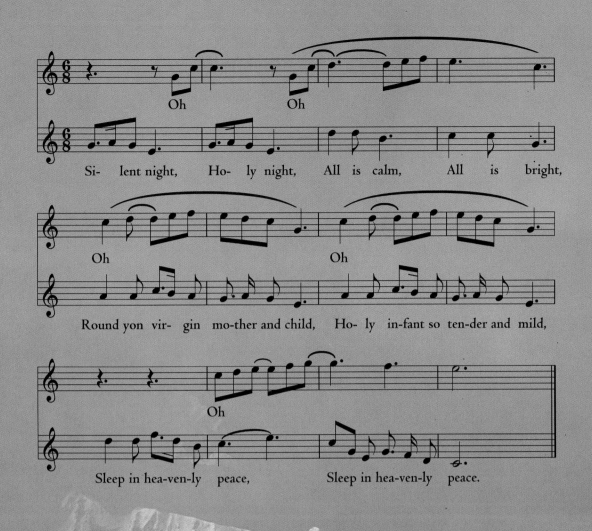

Lyrics and music by Franz Gruber, descant by Duain Wolfe

Sunrise above the Gore Range

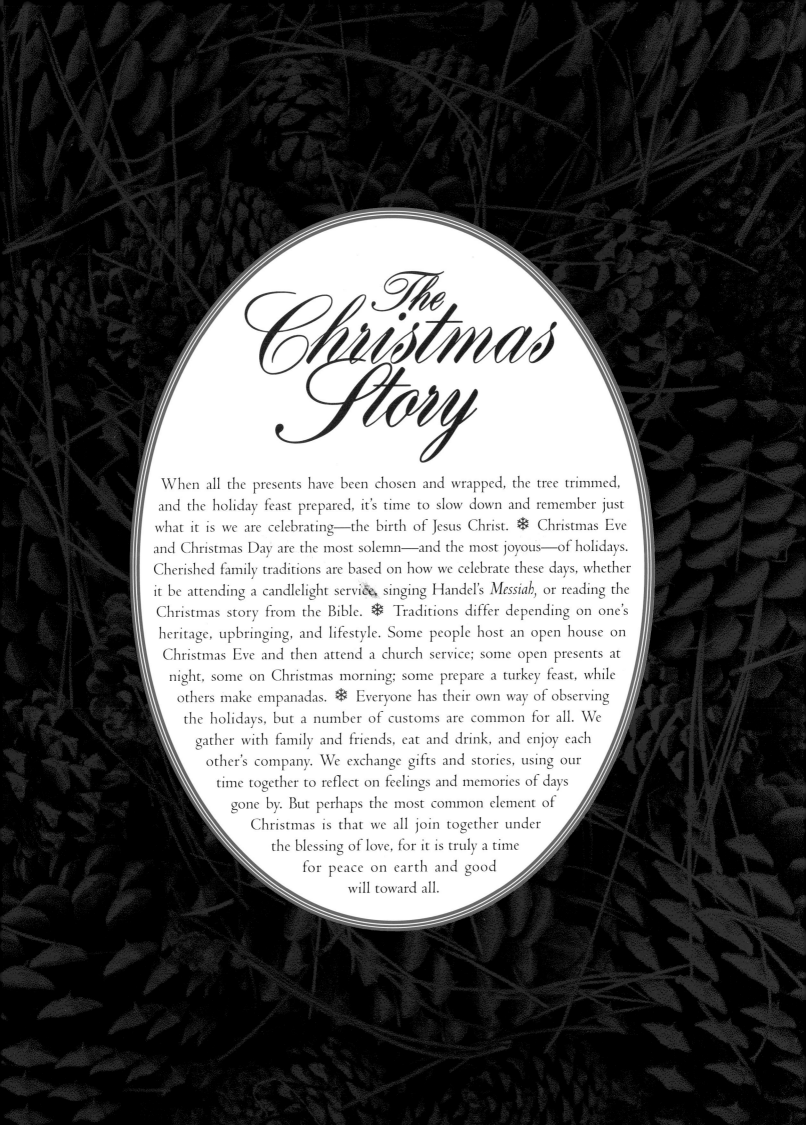

The Christmas Story

When all the presents have been chosen and wrapped, the tree trimmed, and the holiday feast prepared, it's time to slow down and remember just what it is we are celebrating—the birth of Jesus Christ. ❋ Christmas Eve and Christmas Day are the most solemn—and the most joyous—of holidays. Cherished family traditions are based on how we celebrate these days, whether it be attending a candlelight service, singing Handel's *Messiah,* or reading the Christmas story from the Bible. ❋ Traditions differ depending on one's heritage, upbringing, and lifestyle. Some people host an open house on Christmas Eve and then attend a church service; some open presents at night, some on Christmas morning; some prepare a turkey feast, while others make empanadas. ❋ Everyone has their own way of observing the holidays, but a number of customs are common for all. We gather with family and friends, eat and drink, and enjoy each other's company. We exchange gifts and stories, using our time together to reflect on feelings and memories of days gone by. But perhaps the most common element of Christmas is that we all join together under the blessing of love, for it is truly a time for peace on earth and good will toward all.

Behold, a virgin shall conceive, and bear a son,
and shall call his name Immanuel.

— Isaiah 7:14

The Story of Christmas

*And it came to pass in those days, that there went out
a decree from Caesar Augustus, that all the world
should be taxed.*

*(And this taxing was first made when Cyrenius
was governor of Syria.)*

And all went to be taxed, every one into his own city.

*And Joseph also went up from Galilee, out of the city
of Nazareth, into Judea, unto the city of David,
which is called Bethlehem, (because he was of
the house and lineage of David,)*

*To be taxed with Mary his espoused wife,
being great with child.*

*And so it was, that, while they were there, the days
were accomplished that she should be delivered.*

*And she brought forth her firstborn son, and wrapped
him in swaddling clothes, and laid him in a manger;
because there was no room for them in the inn.*

— Luke 2:1-7

*And there were in the same country shepherds
abiding in the field, keeping watch over their
flock by night.*

*And, lo, the angel of the Lord came upon them,
and the glory of the Lord shone round about them;
and they were sore afraid.*

*And the angel said unto them, Fear not: for,
behold, I bring you good tidings of great joy, which
shall be to all people.*

*For unto you is born this day in the city of David
a Saviour, which is Christ the Lord.*

St. Aloysius Church, near Trinidad

And this shall be a sign unto you; Ye shall find the babe wrapped in swaddling clothes, lying in a manger.

And suddenly there was with the angel a multitude of the heavenly host praising God, and saying,

Glory to God in the highest, and on earth peace, good will toward men.

— Luke 2:8-14

AND LAID
HIM

IN A
MANGER

St. John's Church in the Wilderness

*And it came to
pass, as the angels
were gone away
from them into
heaven, the
shepherds said one
to another, Let us
now go even unto Bethlehem, and see this thing which is come
to pass, which the Lord hath made known unto us.*

*And they came with haste, and found Mary and Joseph,
and the babe lying in a manger.*

*And when they had seen it, they made known abroad
the saying which was told them concerning this child.*

*And all they that heard it wondered at those things
which were told them by the shepherds.*

*But Mary kept all these things, and
pondered them in her heart.*

*And the shepherds returned, glorifying and
praising God for all the things that they had
heard and seen, as it was told unto them.*

— Luke 2:15-20

*For unto us a child is born, unto us a son
is given: and the government shall be upon
his shoulder: and his name shall be called
Wonderful, Counselor, The mighty God,
The everlasting Father, The Prince of Peace.*

— Isaiah 9:6

Christmas Eve candlelight services are especially meaningful. While not all Christmas Eve services are candlelit, many Coloradans still list attending church on Christmas Eve and Christmas Day as the most significant part of their celebration. This seems to be true for all generations and denominations.

We asked people what it was about the Christmas season that made their celebrations particularly special. The following comments express some of their thoughts and feelings.

Ouray

Ryssby Church, Longmont

Simpich Character Dolls

We go to our Christmas Eve service, then come home and take turns opening our gifts while we eat snacks.

— L.K., Burlington

The Christmas Eve service at St. John's Cathedral is outstanding—the decorations, the tower bells, and the choirs.

— J.F.L., Englewood

Christmas Eve Eucharist with all the beautiful liturgy and organ music, choir, bell choir and singing congregation, are special to us.

— L.C., Greeley

We attend and participate in the local presentation of the Messiah.

— The M.F. Family, Steamboat Springs

*Historic churches in
Lake City and Ouray*

We have a special reading
of Gospel account on
Christmas Eve
after dinner.

— The K.B. Family,
Parker

Our tradition is to give out
the presents on Christmas
Eve, then attend a church
service. On Christmas
Day we have a big family
Christmas dinner after
attending church again.

— B.M., Ouray

Reading the scriptural
account of the Nativity
on Christmas Eve makes
our Christmas special.

— The R.B. Family,
Lakewood

Midnight Mass at the
Holy Ghost Catholic
Church in Denver is a
must for us. They have
a magnificent choir!

— C.L.,
Red Feather Lakes

Singing carols at our
candlelit Christmas
Eve service is how
we celebrate.

— D.N.,
Manitou Springs

We attended Messiah
concerts in college before
we were married. Now,
if we cannot attend a
performance during the
holiday season, we listen
to a tape while driving to
our holiday destination.

— P.S., Denver

Moore Family Christmas

Our celebration includes family, neighbors, and others who live in our remote mountain town and who have no relatives nearby. We always host an open house after Christmas Eve church services. We serve finger foods and our version of English wassail, which is simmered from early afternoon until the party starts, filling the house with a rich, spicy smell. Since the gathering has become such a long-standing tradition, our guests often bring their own favorite Christmas goodies as well, so there is a wonderful spread. We usually have about 80 people, many of whom remain to sip wassail and visit until nearly midnight.

Coming together out of the snow and cold and celebrating the joy of Christmas with others reminds us of the true sharing aspect of Christmas.

— Charles, Penny, Travis, and Suzanne Moore, Silverton

Moore's Christmas Eve Wassail

3 12-ounce cans apple juice, frozen
1 12-ounce can lemonade, frozen
1 12-ounce can orange juice, frozen
1 12-ounce can pineapple juice, frozen

1½ teaspoons ground cloves
1 stick cinnamon
2 sliced oranges

Place all of the ingredients except the oranges in a large pot at midday and add enough water to make 2½ gallons of wassail. Wait a while and taste, adding ½ to ¾ cup sugar if necessary to sweeten. Simmer over low heat all day. One hour before serving add the sliced oranges. Makes about 50 six-ounce servings.

Blessing Bread

This is called "blessing bread" because it's meant to be given away— a "blessing" to others. It's extraordinarily good banana bread!

¾ cup shortening
⅓ cup vegetable oil
3 large eggs
1½ cups brown sugar
¾ cup white sugar
1 cup bananas, mashed
½ cup chopped nuts (optional)

1 teaspoon vanilla
1 teaspoon baking soda
1 teaspoon baking powder
¾ teaspoon cinnamon
1½ cups zucchini, grated
2½ cups flour

Mix first five ingredients. When the sugars and oil are well creamed, add bananas and vanilla. Mix well. Blend in baking soda, powder, and cinnamon. When all is blended, mix in zucchini, flour, and nuts. Grease and flour 3 loaf pans and line the bottoms with waxed paper. Bake at 350 degrees for 55 to 60 minutes. Makes 3 loaves.

— Lynn Cave

...and lo, the star, which they saw in the east, went before them, till it came and stood over where the young child was.

When they saw the star, they rejoiced with exceeding great joy.

And when they were come into the house, they saw the young child with Mary his mother, and fell down, and worshipped him: and when they had opened their treasures, they presented unto him gifts; gold, and frankincense, and myrrh.

And being warned of God in a dream that they should not return to Herod, they departed into their own country another way.

— Matthew 2:9-12

Cooper Family Christmas

Our family Christmas tradition was going back to my grandparent's farm. We always hung icicles on the tree for there was no snow in the south! I remember lots and lots of presents—not expensive ones but each wrapped separately and opened Christmas morning.

My husband grew up in Argentina, where Christmas is in the middle of summer. Gifts were not given in Argentina on Christmas, but on January 6th children set their shoes outside the door and a present was found in them the next morning.

Simpich Character Dolls

Now, as then, we open presents after eating breakfast and reading the Christmas story from the Bible. Adapting to our American tradition was an adjustment for my husband. He has now, however, discovered the wonderful joy of gift giving.

— Jean Cooper, Littleton

We open one gift Christmas Eve around the tree, then we wake up early to open gifts and see what Santa left during the night. Then we have a huge Christmas dinner with the whole family, or as many as can make it.

— P.M., Denver

When the children were younger, they acted out the Christmas story using the Nativity characters and then we opened our gifts.

— C.M., Englewood

On December 24 we open the gifts and set up nativities from all over the world. I have collected 55 sets.

— R.H., Colorado Springs

Cornice at sunrise, Oh-Be-Joyful Wilderness

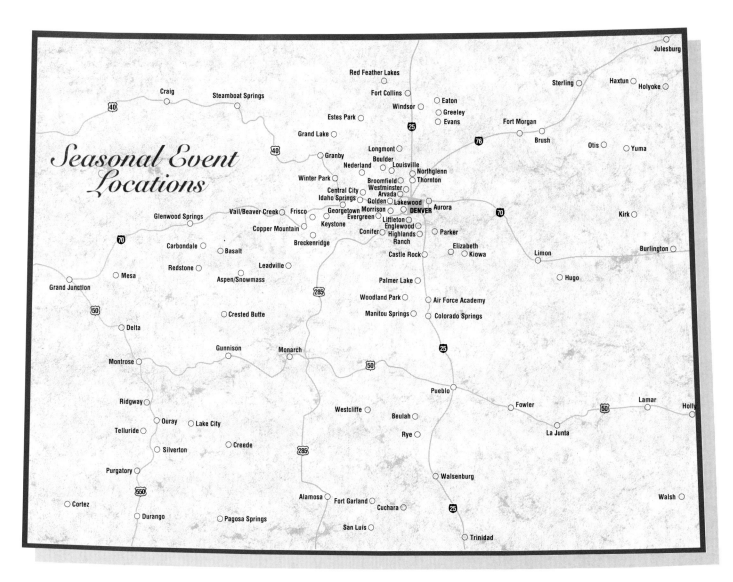

Seasonal Event Locations

COLORADO SKI COUNTRY USA
1560 Broadway, Suite 1440
Denver, CO 80202
(303) 837-0793
(303) 831-SNOW (snow report)

ARROWHEAD AT VAIL SKI MOUNTAIN
Vail, CO 81658
(800) 322-3029

ASPEN HIGHLANDS
Aspen, CO 81611
(800) 356-8811

ASPEN SKIING COMPANY
Aspen, CO 81612
(303) 925-1220

BRECKENRIDGE SKI AREA
Breckenridge, CO 80424
(303) 453-5000

SKI COOPER
Leadville, CO 80461
(719) 486-3684

COPPER MOUNTAIN RESORT
Copper Mountain, CO 80443
(303) 968-2882

CRESTED BUTTE MOUNTAIN RESORT
Mt. Crested Butte, CO 81225
(303) 349-2333

CUCHARA VALLEY SKI RESORT
Cuchara, CO 81055
(719) 742-3163

ELDORA MOUNTAIN RESORT
Nederland, CO 80466
(303) 440-8700

HOWELSEN SKI AREA
Steamboat Springs, CO 80477
(303) 879-4300

KEYSTONE RESORT/ARAPAHOE BASIN
Keystone, CO 80435
(303) 468-4123

LOVELAND SKI AREAS
Georgetown, CO 80444
(303) 569-3203

MONARCH SKI RESORT
Monarch, CO 81227
(719) 539-2581

MOUNTAIN CLIFF SKI RESORT
Westcliffe, CO 81252
(719) 783-2100

POWDERHORN RESORT
Mesa, CO 81643
(303) 245-1140

PURGATORY-DURANGO SKI RESORT
Durango, CO 81301
(303) 247-9000

SILVERCREEK
Granby, CO 80446
(303) 887-3384

STEAMBOAT SKI & RESORT CORPORATION
Steamboat Springs, CO 80487
(303) 879-6111

SKI SUNLIGHT
Glenwood Springs, CO 81601
(303) 945-7491
(800) 445-7931

TELLURIDE SKI RESORT
Telluride, CO 81435
(303) 728-3856

VAIL/BEAVER CREEK RESORT
Vail, CO 81658
(303) 949-5750

WINTER PARK RESORT
Winter Park, CO 80482
(303) 726-5514

WOLF CREEK SKI AREA
Pagosa Springs, CO 81147
(303) 264-5629

Phone numbers listed are the information numbers. To find out more, contact the specific area. Listings are provided by Colorado Ski Country USA.

Seasonal Events

For you to enjoy your own Colorado Kind of Christmas, we have included the following annual events. They are listed alphabetically by city and then by the month in which they occur. This is not intended to be a complete list, but a reference to the type of Christmas activities featured in each area. While every effort has been made to accurately list these events, they are always subject to change. Please refer to the local chambers of commerce and trade associations or to specific arts and humanities organizations for current event information.

ALAMOSA
November
Christmas Lighting Festival

ARVADA
November
Arvada Center Christmas Fair

ASPEN/SNOWMASS
November
Hotel Jerome, 1889 Opening Celebration
Red Brick School House, Holiday Bazaar
Snowmass, Colorado Christmas Crafts Bazaar
December
Anderson Ranch, Holiday Open House
Sardy House Tree Lighting Ceremony
Silvertree Hotel Annual Tree Lighting Ceremony
Snowmass Torchlight Parade down Fanny Hill with Santa
The Wheeler Opera House, Aspen Ballet Company and School, *The Nutcracker*
Wheeler-Stallard House Museum Open House
New Year's Eve
Snowmass Conference Center, Gala Ball
January
Aspen/Snowmass Winterskol Carnival

AURORA
November
Gully Homestead House, Holidays at the Homestead
December
Aurora Dance Arts, *The Nutcracker*

BEULAH
December
Deck the Hall Party
Yule Log Hunt

BOULDER
November
University of Colorado, Boulder Philharmonic Orchestra, *The Nutcracker*
December
Historic Boulder, Homes for the Holiday House Tour
University of Colorado, Festival of Christmas
New Year's Day
Polar Bear Club

BRECKENRIDGE
November
Breckenridge Classic Street Party
Hot Air Balloon Continental Divide Festival
December
Breckenridge Music Institute, Bach, Beethoven and Bon Appetite
Briggle House Summit Historical Society Gathering
Lighting of Breckenridge
Old Fashioned Christmas Month Long Events
Old Fashioned Christmas Home Tour
Winter Series Concerts
January
American International Snow Sculpture Championships
Ullr Fest, Parade, Ball, and World Cup Freestyle Championships

BURLINGTON
November
Open House Christmas
December
Carousel Christmas
Christmas Through a Child's Eyes
Christmas Walk at Old Town
Live Nativity
Parade of Lights
Sing in The Holiday

CASTLE ROCK
November
Annual Star Lighting Ceremony

CENTRAL CITY
November
Wintershire Tours

COLORADO SPRINGS
November
A Colorado Christmas at The Broadmoor
The Broadmoor Annual White Light Tree Lighting Ceremony
Colorado Springs Symphony, Winter Springs Fantasy
Pikes Peak Center, *The Nutcracker*
Simpich Marionettes, *A Christmas Carol*
December
Colorado Springs Symphony, the Broadmoor Skating Club, "Christmas Pops on Ice"
Downtown, Festival of Lights Tree Lighting and Parade
Old Colorado City, Old Fashioned Christmas
Seven Falls, Christmas Lighting at the Falls
White House Ranch, Historic Christmas Celebration
New Year's Eve
AdAmAn Club, Hike to the Top and Pikes Peak Midnight Fireworks

CONIFER
November
Christmas Boutique/Arts & Crafts Fair

COPPER MOUNTAIN
December
Christmas Eve Torchlight Parade and Fireworks
Santa Claus Skis Copper Mountain
Snowboard Series
New Year's Eve
Fireworks

CORTEZ
December
Parade of Lights

CRAIG
November
City Decorates for Christmas
Parade of Christmas Lights
December
Toys for Tots Collection
Hall of Lights

CREEDE
November
Chocolate Festival
December
Christmas in Creede
January
Historical Ball

CRESTED BUTTE
December
Christmas Week Celebration

DELTA
November
Craft Fair
December
Parade of Lights

DENVER METROPOLITAN AREA
November
ArtReach Festival of Trees
Currigan Hall, Annual Holiday Food and Gift Festival
Denver Botanic Gardens, Holiday Sale
Junior League of Denver, Holiday Mart
Museum of Miniatures, Dolls and Toys, Annual Christmas Exhibit
Performing Arts Complex, The Denver Center Theatre Company, *A Christmas Carol*
December
Bromwell House Tour
Central City Opera Guild, L'Esprit de Noel Annual Home Tour
Colorado Ballet, *The Nutcracker*
Colorado Children's Chorale, Christmas Concerts
Colorado Symphony Orchestra, the Colorado Symphony Chorus with the Colorado Children's Chorale, Christmas Pops Concerts
Colorado Symphony Orchestra, Colorado Symphony Chorus, Handel's *Messiah*
Denver Botanic Gardens, Blossoms of Light

Denver Botanic Gardens, Teddy
Bear Teas
Denver Center Theatre
Company, *A Christmas Carol*
Denver Zoo, Wild Lights
Downtown Denver Partnership,
Inc., News 4 Parade of Lights
Four Mile Historic Park,
Holiday Open House
Governor's Mansion, Holiday
Tours
Grant-Humphreys Mansion/
Byers-Evans House, Evening
Tours
Holidays at the Ice House
Larimer Square Christmas Walk
Lighting of the Denver City and
County Building
Molly Brown House, Victorian
Christmas
Museum of Miniatures, Dolls
and Toys, Candlelight Tours

New Year's Eve
Colorado Symphony Orchestra,
New Year's Eve Sparkler
First Night Colorado

January
Colorado Indian Market and
Western Roundup
The National Western Stock
Show & Rodeo

DURANGO
November
Caroling Procession and
Lighting Ceremony
Durango & Silverton Narrow
Gauge Railroad, Winter
Holidays on the Silverton

December
A Durango Christmas—How
They Did It In 1891
Art Ole
Boulevard Neighborhood
Association Luminaria
Christmas Light Tour
Merchant Window Decorating
Contest
Strater Hotel, Diamond Circle
Theater, The Joy of
Christmas
Toys for Tots Collection

EATON
December
Chamber of Commerce
Christmas Party
Christmas House Tours
Santa Lucia Festival

ELBERT
November
Craft Fair

ELIZABETH
December
Christmas Fair
Elizabethan Christmas
Santa Claus Parade

ESTES PARK
November
Art Center, The Holiday
Collection
Come Catch the Glow Christmas
Parade
Stanley Hotel Concert Series
Teddy Bear Christmas Annual
Holiday House

December
Estes Park Music Festival,
Colorado Children's Chorale
Estes Park Chorale, Round the
Table Sing
Stanley Hotel Concert Series

EVANS
November
Fall/Christmas Bazaar

EVERGREEN
December
Winterfest Evergreen

FORT COLLINS
November
Lincoln Center, *Nutcracker* ballet

December
Colorado State Forest Service
tree cutting weekends

FORT GARLAND
December
Fort Garland Museum, Festival
of Lights

FORT MORGAN
November
Christmas Bazaar and Vision of
Trees

December
Fort Morgan Christmas Parade

FOWLER
December
Christmas Posada

FRISCO
December
Old Fashioned Christmas

GEORGETOWN
December
Christmas at Hamill House
Christmas Market
Santa's Express Train

GLENWOOD SPRINGS
December
Luminaria Lighting Celebration
and Candlelight Holiday
Walk
Mountain Madrigal Singers,
Christmas Concert

GOLDEN
December
DAR Pioneer Museum, Lighting
Ceremony
Foothills Art Center, Annual
Holiday Art Market
Railroad Museum, Steam Up
Santa Claus Train

GRAND JUNCTION
November
Cross Orchards Children's
Christmas Workshop
Crafty Peddlar Christmas Fair

December
Cross Orchards Annual Country
Christmas
Parade of Lights

GRAND LAKE
November
Old Fashioned Christmas Arts
and Crafts Bazaar

December
Community Caroling
Holiday Melodrama
Live Nativity Play
Old Fashioned Christmas

New Year's Eve
Fireworks

January
Snowmobile Drag Racing
Winter Carnival Ice Sculptures
Winter Carnival Snow Parade

GREELEY
November
Annual Downtown Lighting
Ceremony
Yuletide Treasures Fine Arts and
Crafts Sale

December
Monfort Concert Hall,
Poinsettia Pops Concert
Festival of Trees
Greeley Chorale Madrigal Feast
Northern Lights Events
Northern Lights at Centennial
Village
University of Northern
Colorado, Choirs Christmas
Concert

January
Colorado Farm Show

GUNNISON
December
Christmas Parade and Christmas
Tree Lighting

HAXTUN
December
Christmas Lights Lighting with
Soup Supper

HOLLY
December
Christmas City Fun
Christmas Card Remailing

HOLYOKE
November
Chamber Christmas Lights
Lighting and Chili Supper
Holly Daze Craft Fair

HUGO
December
Living Christmas Tree Cantata

IDAHO SPRINGS
December
Christmas Tree Lighting

JULESBURG
November
Craft Fair
Julesburg Chili Feed and
Christmas Lighting

KEYSTONE
December
Annual Tree Trimming Party
and Christmas Caroling
Cross Country Moonlight Tour
Keystone's Costumed Characters
Ice Skating on Keystone Lake
Santa Claus Visits the Village

New Year's Eve
Annual Gala

KIOWA
December
Old Fashioned Christmas in
Kiowa

LA JUNTA
December
Bent's Old Fort, 1846 Christmas
Koshare Winter Ceremonial

LAKE CITY
December
Chamber of Commerce
Community Pot Luck and
Caroling
Christmas School Play
Community Choir Christmas
Concert

New Year's Eve
Mayor's Celebration

LAMAR
November
Chamber of Commerce,
    Enchanted Forest Christmas
    Lights
December
Two Shot Goose Hunt

LIMON
December
Christmas Promotion
Christmas Tree Walk Festival
Christmas Vespers

LITTLETON
November
Candlelight Walk and Tree
    Lighting Ceremony

LONGMONT
December
Adopt-a-Tree Program
Holiday on Main Street
Holiday Parade of Lights
Longmont Museum, Children's
    Holiday Party

LOUISVILLE
December
Holiday Festival of Lights
    Parade
Louisville Center for the Arts,
    Young Artists Exhibit

MANITOU SPRINGS
November
Miramont Castle Victorian
    Christmas
December
Christmas Walk

MONARCH
December
Santa Skis Monarch
New Year's Eve
Evening of Light & Torchlight
    Parade

MONTROSE
November
Annual Craft Show and Sale
December
Chocolate Lovers Affair
Christmas Parade

OTIS
December
Santa on the Plains Christmas
    Eve

OURAY
December
Elks Annual Christmas Eve
    Santa Visits
Ouray County Museum, A
    Child's Victorian Christmas

PAGOSA SPRINGS
December
Community Holiday Party
Liberty Theatre, Children's
    Holiday Matinee
Tree Lighting Ceremony

PALMER LAKE
December
Yule Log Festival

PUEBLO
November
Holiday Craft Boutiques
Rosemount Victorian Christmas,
    A Dickens of a Christmas
Town and Gown Performance
    Series
December
Christmas Parade of Lights
Christmas Posada
El Pueblo Museum, Living
    Christmas of the 1840's
Pueblo Ballet performances of
    The Nutcracker
Rosemount House Tea with
    Santa
Rosemount Victorian Christmas
    Series
Sangre de Cristo Center Festival
    of Trees
Spirit of Christmas Past
State Fairgrounds, Christmas
    Season Fair
January
Pueblo Symphony Concerts

PURGATORY
December
Christmas Celebration
New Year's Eve
Fireworks and Torchlight Parade

REDSTONE
November
Grand Illumination

RIDGWAY
November
Ridgway Tree Lighting and
    Caroling Party

RYE
December
Bishop Castle, Christmas at the
    Castle

SAN LUIS
December
Fiesta de Nuestra Senora de
    Guadalupe
Las Posadas
January
Tres Reyes

SILVERTON
November
Christmas Bazaar
December
Yule Log Festival

STEAMBOAT SPRINGS
November
Benefit Day
December
Christmas in the Rockies
    Holiday Market
Columbine Chorale's Christmas
    Concert
Howelsen Hill, Annual
    Christmas Town Party
Mountain Madrigal Singers,
    Olde English Madrigal
    Dinners
Ski Ball
Strings in the Mountains
    Holiday Concerts
New Year's Eve
Torchlight Parade
January
Winterworks Art Invitational

STERLING
November
St. Anthony's Bazaar
December
Arts Council Christmas Program
Sterling Court House Christmas
    Lighting

TELLURIDE
November
Sheridan Opera House, *The
    Nutcracker* ballet
Telluride Winter Jazz
    Festival/Winter Festival
    Series
December
Christmas Eve Torchlight
    Parade
DecemberFest/Winter Festival
    Series
Elks Children's Christmas Party
Firemen's Christmas Tree
    Lighting on Main Street
Noel Night
The Telluride Museum,
    Victorian Christmas
New Year's Eve
Firemen's Ball
New Year's Eve Torchlight
    Parade
January
Annual Butch Cassidy Cross-
    Country Chase

TRINIDAD
December
Baca House Candlelight Tours

**UNITED STATES AIR FORCE
ACADEMY**
November
Cadet Chorale, Handel's *Messiah*
December
Operation Christmas
Festival of Lessons and Carols
Academy Band Christmas
    Concerts

VAIL/BEAVER CREEK
November
Annual Holiday Fair
Festival of Lights
Vail Mountain School Auction
The Spirit of the Season—A
    Festival of Foods
December
Annual Tree Lightings at Vail,
    Beaver Creek and Lionshead
Avon's Christmas Party
Betty Ford Alpine Gardens,
    Winter Interlude
Crystal Ball
Dobson Ice Arena, Christmas
    Show
Festival of Lights
New Year's Eve
New Year's Eve Fireworks
Teen Party

WALSH
December
Walsh Art Center, Christmas
    Dinner Theatre

WINDSOR
November
Christmas in Windsor Craft Fair

WINTER PARK
November
Rio Grande Ski Train, Denver to
    Winter Park Resort
December
Christmas Eve Torchlight
    Parade
Ski With Santa at Silvercreek

WOODLAND PARK
December
Arts and Crafts Fair

YUMA
November
Christmas Tree Lighting
December
Elfville Santa's Workshop
Gingerbread Baking and House
    Decorating Contest

*W*e especially thank the following for their assistance and valuable expertise in the research and development of *A Colorado Kind of Christmas.*

AAA COLORADO
4100 E. Arkansas Avenue
Denver, CO 80222
(303) 753-8800
Ronald C. Collier, President
and General Manager

COLORADO CHILDREN'S CHORALE
910 15th Street
Suite 1020
Denver, CO 80202
(303) 892-5600
Duain Wolfe, Artistic
Director and Conductor

EPICUREAN CATERING
469 S. Cherry Street
Suite 120
Denver, CO 80222
(303) 321-0343
Larry DiPasquale, President

All Seasons Carriage Service
Association of Historic
Hotels of the Rocky
Mountain West
Brown Palace Hotel
C & G Publishing, Inc.
C Lazy U Ranch
Castle Marne
Christmas Shop
Cleveholm Manor
Cosolo's Italian Market
Crystal Farm
Denver Buffalo Company
Durango & Silverton Narrow
Gauge Railroad
Floradora Restaurant
Geoffrey Fowler Salon
Goldsmith's Salon
Holly Berry House
Jack Southard, Inc.
John Dillon Music
Krabloonik
Lemmon Lodge
Merrit House
Mount Elbert Lodge Bed &
Breakfast
Mountain Lake Properties
North Pole
Norwest Banks

Ouray Variety Store
Quick Copy
Redstone Inn
Reed Photo
Ridgway Land Company
Rutherford Carriage Service
Scrooge & Marley Ltd.
Simpich Character Dolls
Sturgeon Electric Company,
Inc.
T-Lazy-7 Ranch
Tanner, Dirks & Co, Inc.
The Aurora Potter's Guild
The Broadmoor
The Christmas Cottage
The Cristmas Store
The Dickens Carolers
The Fort Restaurant
The Oxford Hotel
The Seasoned Chef
The Silverton Standard
The Silvertree Hotel
Tradition
Winding River Resort

*T*hank you to all who have supported this project. Many have generously shared their stories, their recipes, and their traditions. Many others have shared their time and expertise.

Margaret Aarestad
Dennis and Carol Ahnen
Sally Anderson
Susan Anderson
Jane Andrade
Jeanette Armburstmacher
Kathy Van Arsdale
Rosa L. Ashby
Robert Babb
Jim Bain
Donna Baker
Roberta Bargman
Barbara Bauerle
Mary Kay Barkus
Bonnie Beach
Lynn Beach
Sue Beasley
Richard E. Bennett Sr. Family
Marilyn Beman
Esther Bensik
Richard and Twila Bird Family
Connie Birdsong
Jim and Phoebe Bishop
Sue Bissell
Suzy Blackhurst
Kerry and Barbara Blount
Jack and Natalie Blumenthal
Joanne Bolnick
Susie Bolton
Christine Bradley
Jeannene Bragg
Linda Brancato
B. George Braniff
Madalyn Brogan
Jane Brown
Michelle Bruning
Jane Bullock
Frances M. Burch
Mary Louise Burke
Donna Burns
John Calhoun
Debbie Callender
Lois Camp
Carol Bliss Cannon
Marie Carlson
Robert Carlson Family
Stacy Carson

Lynn Cave
Betsy Chalender
Patricia Champion
Bonnie Champion
Joan Chatfield
Chris Chavez
Dianne Chrismer
Susan Christiansen
Leanna Clark
Frankie L. Clark
Barbara J. Clayton
Bill Coburn
Debbie Coffey
Tara M. Colee
Susan Coleman
Dawn Ernest Cone
Barbara A. Conrad
Sandi Cook
Davis and Jean Cooper
Mary E. Cornish
Gary Covert
Elwin and Annie Crabtree
Gary Crawford
Claudia Cupp
Linda Dalton
Katy Daniel
Ray Daniel
Warren and Simie Daniel
Warren and Dottie Daniel
William Daniel, Jr.
William Daniel
Gertrude Davis
David Davis
Jesse Dawson
Christine D. Dawson
Emily Dawson
Joe, Debbie, Amy, and Julie DeBartolo
Michelle DeFrange
Jim DeMersman
Margaret DeMichelis
Pam Dennis
Deborah DeSantis
George Devers
Noah Dickson
Deborah Dickson
Jim Diehl
Lorijo Dietmeier

Anne Dirks
David Dirks
Katherine Dirks
Michael Dirks
Vera B. Dirks
Barb Doerr
Jan Donato
Kathy Donnelly
Corry Doty
Jo Downey
George C. Downing
Susan Dreyer
Ruth Dusenberg
Sandra L. Dyer
Allyson Eccles
Stephanie Ehret
Pelle and Chris Eklund
Nancy Eriksen
Deborah Espinosa
Stacy Everhart
Mario Ewell
Wayne and Sarah Eye
K. Fallert
Jim Felton
Kathy Fiebig
Mark Fischer Family
John Fisher Family
Lynda Fisher
Renee Flinn
Former Grinch of Christmas
Liz Frawley
Alva Gallegos
R. Louis Gavioli Family
Gail Gerard
Leslie Gerarden
Milli Girard
Golden Girl
Dian Goldberg
Marjorie H. Goldstein
Grant and Klea Goodson
Wendy Gordon
Suzi Gossard
Justin Gossard
Brandon Gossard
Shannon Gossard
Julie Gosswiller
Kevin Gramer
Nancy Schroeder Grant
Betse Grassby

Jack and Judy Green
Cindy Greene
Leah Greksa
Susan Grupe
Reina Gutierrez
Nick and Anne Hackstock
Susan Hagar
Bob Hand
David Hanley
Linda Hanson
Richard Hartman Family
Joan Harden
Cheryl Hardy-Moore
Richard Harvey
Rick, Diane, Jessica, and Lauren Hassett
Steve Hatfield
Alvin and Magdalen Havekost
Linda Hawthorne
Dick and Penny Hayes
Jo Anne Haynes
Nancy Hegsted
Janet Heisz
Marcia Hansen Helling
Barbara Henning-Martinez
Marcia Henry
Tim Henry
Erin Hess
Frances Ellen Hewitt
Charles Hickman Family
Nancy Hiester
Lisa A. Higbee
Geneva Hill
Kristi L. Hill
George and Susan Hills
Tom Hines
Wes and Sue House
Pat Howard
Dianne Howie
Richard H. Huerta
Pam Hueseman
R.G. and Carlita Huff
Corinne Hunt
Catherine Hutchinson
Gwen Ippen
Patsy Isham
Lynna Jackson

V. Jacobson
Ted and Sue James
Betty Janssen
Jackie Jaquint
Jim Jarman
Carole Jenny
Claire Jessee
Marvin and Judy Johnson
Nancy Johnson
S.A. Johnson
Greg Johnson
Brewster and Linda Johnson
Dave and Margie Johnson
Todd Johnson
Darrell and Leah Jones
Eric Jones
Ian Jones
Elizabeth D. Jones
Trevor Jones
Mary Joslin
Mary Joss
Laurie Kahler
Martha Kelce
Patience Cairns Kemp
Shannon Kennedy
Stephen Kent
Heidi Keogh
Michael Keye
Tammy Kibler
Jan Kiefer
Betty Kilsdonk
Amy Kimberly
Bob and Bev King
Frank Kirschbaum
Jorge O. Klajnbart Family
Kristen Koehler
Shannon Koehler
David and Vicki Koehler
Sherri Koelbel
Lisa Konrad
Kristen Kopplin
Jan Koppri
Kimberly Koppri
J.R. Kowaleswki
Ruth Krauss
Mary Krewson
Cathy Kruzic
Eric and Nancy Kurzweil

Bev and Jay Labe
Todd Lampe
Samuel B. Lancaster
Michael Lane
Charlotte Lauric
Nancy Lavington
Don and Karen Sue
   Lawhead
Addie Lawrence
Fred and Nellie Lawrence
Bill Lee
Sarah Leffen
Parker Lenure
Kay Lenure
Nicole Leshaw
Betty R. Lewis-Labe
Gene and Maureen
   Lienert
Steve and Marilyn
   Lindenbaum
Dianne Lindenmeyer
Barbara Loken
Monique Lopez
Vivian Lowe
Helen Lowrey
Lt. April L. Lubliner
Bill Luetzen
Timothy P. Luksa
Tom Lundell
W. Thomas Lundell
John Luzader
Daryl and Karen
   MacCarter
Dan MacEachen
Megan Mackenzie
Joan Maclachlan
Ken and Sue Majeski
Stefan Majeski
Jody Maliga-LeJeune and
   Family
Cheryl Malina
Dustin Malina
Paula Manini
Kerry Manion
Mark Mantzke
Pauline Marshall
Tom and Cydney
   Marsico
Julie Martin
Elizabeth Marvin
Kristina Maxfield
Gail McBride
Louis McBurney
Jody McCabe
Molly McCarthy
Patti McCarthy

Elizabeth McCarthy
Chris McCauley
Michael McClure
Therese McClure
Nicole McGown
Leslie McKay
Ed McKeever
Michael N. McKenna
Christina A. McLean
Pat McMullin
Mardi McTeer
Carol Meisenheimer
Ken Meredith Family
Ann Hatfield Merritt
Ed and Kay Messenger
Judith Metcalfe
Richard Metzski
Lucy Meyring
Ralph and Peggy Miller
Mary Kay Mitchell
Posey Moller
Mike and Janice Moore
Charles, Penny, Travis,
   and Suzanne Moore
Loretta Morgan
Shirley Morrison
John and Jean Moseley
   Family
Sally Mundell
Barbara L. Muntyan
David Murphy
Susan Murray
Cliff and Debi
   Nancarrow
Richard and Michelle
   Navarre
Rick and Peggy Naylor
Ronald J. Neely
Danielle D. Nelson
Darrel E. Nelson
Diane Newcom
Mary Ann Nichols
Pamela Nocerino
Susan Noltemeyer
Diane Nowak
Blake Nuccio
Pat Oestereicher
Barbara O'Grady
Barry Oliver
Susan Olson
Alyssa Orndorf
Joshua Orndorf
April Orndorf
Hope Ostheimer
Kate Parke
Nancy Parker

Louise V. Parker
Laura Parramore
Vicki Patterson
Julie Payne
Alisan Payne
Fred P. Payne
Gini Pearson
Marilyn Pearson
Becky Perry
Jim and Karen Perry
Bob and Deanna Person
Jane Peterson
Kim Peterson
Annely Peterson
Mary Sue Petticrew
Eileen I. Pfeifer
Sam Winslow Philben
Dan and Judy Polidori
Todd Posinan
Gene Pret
Vincent Pret
Dino Pret
David Putnam
Larry Putnam
Nancy C. Putnam
Deborah Ramsey
Frank and Nellie Rankin
S.M. Raver
Joannie Regester
Edna F. Reid
Aaron Reite
Carolyn Reite
Warren Rempel
Julie Reusser
Robert Reynouard
   Family
Kendra Rhoades
Edith R. Rhodes
Nancy Rice
Myra Rich
Janet M. Richardson
April Richey
Fran Ridgley
Lisa Rigsby
Janet Riley
Richard R. Rizzo
Randy Robbins
Silas Robbins
Lee Robinson
Gayedine Rodriguez
Martha Rodriguez
Hines and Hazel Rogers
Chip and Julie Rogers
Rich Roppa
Hindi Roseman
Jil Rosentnater

Mary Rotola
J. Cooper Rounds
Ruthann Russell
Pat Rustad
Buff and Mary Lou
   Rutherford
Caitlin M. Saling
David M. Saling
Annette D. Saling
Joe and Corrine Sanchez
Bill Saul
James M. Schlarbaum
Debbie Schmit-Lobis
Darlene B. Scott
Bob Scott
Christine Scrip
T. Scruggs
Paulette Shank
Sara Shankland
Kellie Shannon
Joanne B. Shannon
William D. Sharpe
Melanie Shearer
John Sheehan Family
June Simonton
Jill M. Simpson
Shae Singer
Edwin and Frances Sloan
Sandy Smith
Kellen D. Smith
Ronald D. Smith
Larry Solan
Jackie Spacek
Linda Speer
Michael Speer Family
Barbara M. Spencer
Jan Spomer
Nancy Springer
Gully Stanford
Patty L. Stanley
Lis K. Steere
Linda Stephens
Kasia Stevens
Fran Strange
Deborah C. Strom
Jean Strop
Geri Stutheit
Charla Sullivan
Doris Sutton
Lynn Swain
Steve Swanson
Ace Swerdlove
Mary Taitt
Judy Tate
Wendy Wimbush Taylor
Jim and Cindy Tanner

Lindsay Tanner
Julia Rael Tapia
P.C. Tapper
Judy Tate
Mildred P. Teigler
Jim Thompson
Jack and Bonnie Thorne
Eileen Tomaro
Sandy Torres
Sureva Towler
Beatrice Neff Trautman
Chris Tucker
Leslie Tweed
Luanne Unks
Lois Upper
Martha Vair
Kathy VanArsdale
Barbara Van Hook
Mary Vanier
Suzanne Venino
Susan Villano
Linda Vogel
Lynda S. Vogel
Deborah L. Voss
Kendyll Vresilovic
Harry Ward
Stephen and Genie
   Waters
Helle Watson
Mike Way
Robert Wells
Karen Wherley
Joan Wickman
Mary Jean Wiegel
Rosemary Wilkin
Patti Williams
Mary Williams
LaWanna Wilson
Marj Wilson
Frances Wilson
Bill and Marj Wise
Caroline Witty
Duain Wolfe
E.D. Woodring
Robert and Nancy
   Woodward
Ann-Marie Worthington
Frank R. Young
Anthony and Ann
   Zennaiter
Judy Ziegler
Diane Zieroth

…and to all of the
many AAA Colorado
members who responded
to our survey.

Rocky Mountain Resources

Thank you to the many Colorado chambers of commerce, trade associations, arts and humanities organizations, and government agencies who made this book a true reflection of Colorado at Christmastime. Many people helped with the development of this book. They are available to help you with your planning, and we have listed their organizations below.

ASPEN CHAMBER RESORT ASSOCIATION
328 E. Hyman Avenue
Aspen, CO 81612
(303) 925-1940

ASPEN HIGHLANDS SKIING CORPORATION
1600 Maroon Creek Road
Aspen, CO 81611
(303) 925-5300

ASPEN SKIING COMPANY
P.O. Box 1248
Aspen, CO 81612
(303) 925-1220

BASALT CHAMBER OF COMMERCE—MEDC
105 Midland Avenue
Basalt, CO
(303) 927-4031

BRECKENRIDGE SKI CORPORATION
P.O. Box 1058
Breckenridge, CO 80424
(303) 453-5000

BRECKENRIDGE RESORT CHAMBER
P.O. Box 1909
Breckenridge, CO 80424
(303) 453-2913

CASTLE ROCK CHAMBER OF COMMERCE
420 Jerry Street
Castle Rock, CO 80104
(303) 688-4597

CITY OF AURORA, PARKS AND RECREATION
1470 S. Havana Street
Aurora, CO 80012
(303) 344-1776

CITY AND COUNTY OF DENVER
City & County Building
Room 40
Denver, CO 80202
(303) 640-2261 or 640-3386

CITY OF GREELEY
651 10th Avenue
Greeley, CO 80631
(303) 350-9450

CITY OF LOUISVILLE
749 Main Street
Louisville, CO 80027
(303) 666-8331

COLORADO COMMUNITY CHAMBER OF COMMERCE
0590 Highway 133
Carbondale, CO 81623
(303) 963-1890

COLORADO HOTEL & LODGING ASSOCIATION, INC.
999 18th Street, Suite 1240
Denver, CO 80202
(303) 297-8335

COLORADO SKI COUNTRY USA
1560 Broadway, Suite 1440
Denver, CO 80202
(303) 837-0793

COLORADO SPRINGS CONVENTION & VISITORS BUREAU
104 S. Cascade Avenue, Suite 104
Colorado Springs, CO 80903
(719) 635-7506

COLORADO STATE FOREST SERVICE
Colorado State University
   Campus, Forestry Building
Fort Collins, CO 80523
(303) 491-6303

COLORADO TOURISM BOARD
1625 Broadway, Suite 1700
Denver, CO 80202
(303) 592-5410 or
(800) 433-2656

COPPER MOUNTAIN RESORT
P.O. Box 3001
Copper Mountain, CO 80443
(303) 968-2882

CREEDE-MINERAL COUNTY CHAMBER OF COMMERCE
P.O. Box 580
Creede, CO 81130
(719) 658-2374

DOWNTOWN DENVER PARTNERSHIP, INC.
511 16th Street
Denver, CO 80202
(303) 534-6161

DURANGO AREA CHAMBER RESORT ASSOCIATION
P.O. Box 2587
Durango, CO 81302
(303) 247-0312

GLENWOOD SPRINGS CHAMBER RESORT ASSOCIATION
1102 Grand Avenue
Glenwood Springs, CO 81601
(303) 945-6589

GRAND JUNCTION VISITOR & CONVENTION BUREAU
360 Grand Avenue
Grand Junction, CO 81501
(800) 962-2547

GRAND LAKE AREA CHAMBER OF COMMERCE
P.O. Box 57
Grand Lake, CO 80447
(303) 627-3402

GREATER CRAIG AREA CHAMBER OF COMMERCE
360 E. Victory Way
Craig, CO 81625
(303) 824-5689

GREATER DENVER CHAMBER OF COMMERCE
1445 Market Street
Denver, CO 80202-1729
(303) 534-8500

IDAHO SPRINGS CHAMBER OF COMMERCE
P.O. Box 97
Idaho Springs, CO 80452
(303) 567-4382

KEYSTONE RESORT
P.O. Box 38
Keystone, CO 80435
(303) 468-4123

LAKE CITY CHAMBER OF COMMERCE
P.O. Box 430
Lake City, CO 81235
(303) 944-2527

LAKE DILLON RESORT ASSOCIATION
P.O. Box 446
Dillon, CO 80435
(303) 468-6222

LAMAR CHAMBER OF COMMERCE
P.O. Box 1540
Lamar, CO 81052
(719) 336-9095

LONGMONT DOWNTOWN DEVELOPMENT AUTHORITY
528 Main Street
Longmont, CO 80501
(303) 651-8484

MONTROSE COUNTY CHAMBER OF COMMERCE
550 N. Townsend Avenue
Montrose, CO 81401
(303) 249-5515

OLD TOWN MUSEUM & EMPORIUM
420 S. 14th Street
Burlington, CO 80807
(719) 346-7382

OURAY CHAMBER OF COMMERCE
Ouray, CO 81427
(303) 325-4746

PAGOSA SPRINGS AREA CHAMBER OF COMMERCE
P.O. Box 787
Pagosa Springs, CO 81147
(303) 264-2360

PIKES PEAK ARTS COUNCIL
P.O. Box 1073
Colorado Springs, CO 80901
(719) 685-5178

PUEBLO CHAMBER OF
COMMERCE
P.O. Box 697
Pueblo, CO 81002
(800) 233-3446

RIDGWAY VISITOR CENTER
P.O. Box 500
Ridgway, CO 81432
(303) 626-5868

RIFLE CHAMBER OF
COMMERCE
P.O. Box 809
Rifle, CO 81650
(303) 625-2085

SAN LUIS VALLEY ECONOMIC
DEVELOPMENT COUNCIL
P.O. Box 300
Alamosa, CO 81101
(719) 589-7490

STEAMBOAT SPRINGS
CHAMBER RESORT
ASSOCIATION
P.O. Box 774408
Steamboat Springs, CO 80477
(303) 879-0882

TELLURIDE CHAMBER
RESORT ASSOCIATION
P.O. Box 653
Telluride, CO 81435
(303) 728-3041

TELLURIDE SKI RESORT
P.O. Box 1115
Telluride, CO 81435
(303) 728-7404

TOWN OF ESTES PARK
P.O. Box 1967
Estes Park, CO 80517
(800) 443-7837

TOWN OF FRISCO
P.O. Box 4100
Frisco, CO 80443
(303) 668-5276

TOWN OF PALMER LAKE
P.O. Box 208
Palmer Lake, CO 80133
(719) 481-2975

TRINIDAD/LAS ANIMAS
CHAMBER OF COMMERCE
309 Nevada Avenue
Trinidad, CO 81082
(719) 846-928

U.S. AIR FORCE ACADEMY
Colorado 80840-5000
(719) 472-4050

U.S. DEPARTMENT
OF AGRICULTURE
FOREST SERVICE
ROCKY MOUNTAIN REGION
740 Simms
P.O. Box 25127
Lakewood, CO 80225
(303) 236-9431

VAIL RESORT ASSOCIATION
100 E. Meadow Drive
Vail, CO 81657
(303) 476-1000

VAIL VALLEY FOUNDATION
P.O. Box 309
Vail, CO 81658
(303) 476-9500

VAIL VALLEY TOURISM &
CONVENTION BUREAU
100 E. Meadow Drive
Vail, CO 81657
(800) 525-3875

VAIL ASSOCIATES, INC.
P.O. Box 7
Vail, CO 81658
(303) 949-5750

WEST YUMA COUNTY
CHAMBER OF COMMERCE
P.O. Box 383
Yuma, CO 80759
(303) 848-2704

Arts and Humanities Organizations

ArtReach Festival of Trees,
    Denver
ARTS Elizabeth
Aspen Historical Society
Aurora Dance Arts
Baca/Bloom House and
    Pioneer Museum, Trinidad
Beulah Valley Arts Council
Bishop Castle, Rye
Central City Opera House
    Association, Denver
Colorado Symphony
    Orchestra, Denver
Colorado Council on Arts
    and Humanities, Denver
Colorado Ski Museum, Vail
Colorado Ballet, Denver
Columbine Chorale,
    Steamboat Springs
Cross Orchards Historic Site,
    Grand Junction
Cultural Arts Council of
    Estes Park
Denver Public Library
    FRIENDS Foundation
Denver Botanic Gardens
Denver Center Theatre
    Company
Denver Museum of
    Miniatures, Dolls and Toys
Durango Arts Center
El Pueblo Museum, Pueblo
Estes Park Historical
    Museum
Evergreen Area Council for
    the Arts
Four Mile Historic Park,
    Denver
Georgetown Loop Railroad
Grand Lake Arts Council
Grant-Humphreys Mansion,
    Denver
Gully Homestead House,
    Aurora
Hamill House, Georgetown

Historic Georgetown, Inc.
Holly Commercial Club
Holyoke Community Arts
    Council
Keep the Lights Foundation,
    Denver
Kit Carson County Carousel
    Association, Stratton
L'Esprit de Noel Christmas
    Home Tour, Denver
Larimer Square, Denver
Limon Promotions Council
Limon Heritage Society
Longmont Museum
Mile High United Way,
    Denver
Molly Brown House
    Museum, Denver
Mountain Madrigal Singers,
    Steamboat Springs
Museum of Western
    Colorado, Grand Junction
Old Town Museum,
    Burlington
Ouray County Museum
Ouray Lodge No. 492,
    B.P.O.E.
Ryssby Church, Longmont
Sangre de Cristo Arts and
    Conference Center, Pueblo
Silver Plume Singers
Steamboat Springs Arts
    Council
Strings in the Mountains,
    Steamboat Springs
Teller House Museum,
    Central City
Telluride Council for the Arts
    and Humanities
The Children's Museum of
    Denver
The Children's Hospital
    Foundation, Denver
The Denver Center For The
    Performing Arts
The Denver Santa Claus
    Shop, Inc.
Vistas of Time, Loveland
Walsh Art Center, Walsh
Wheeler Opera House, Aspen

Photography

Photography provided by the following:

Affleck, Jack, Vail Associates, Inc., 88 (top right), 89, 96

Ashe, Robert, The Brown Palace, 74 (left)

Bartee, Rob, Keep the Lights Foundation, 82-83

Benson, Joan, Crystal Farm, 31

Brown, Larry, The Stock Broker, 92

C Lazy U Ranch, 52, 93

Cook, James A., The Stock Broker, 41

Downtown Denver Partnership, Inc., James A. Rae, 66-67

Durango & Silverton Narrow Gauge Railroad, Durango Area
    Chamber Resort Assoc., 100 (top)

Fielder, John, 2, 7, 8-9, 10-11, 29, 30, 36, 39 (top), 53, 58, 60,
    84, 86, 91, 102-103, 104, 106, 116-117

Harris, Robert E., St. John's Cathedral Archives, 110

Hubbell, National Western Stock Show & Rodeo, 98, 99

Keystone Resort, 88, 89

Laszlo, Colorado Ballet, 63 (top right)

Litz, Brian, 5, 12, 14, 15, 18, 19, 20, 23, 24, 25, 26, 27, 28, 32,
    35, 39 (small), 42, 45, 46, 51, 55, 57 (all), 63 (singers), 64
    (all), 65 (all), 68, 69 (all), 70 (all), 71, 73, 74 (bottom right),
    75 (top & bottom right), 77, 80 (all), 81 (all), 89 (top 3 &
    bottom) 90, 93 (bottom), 94, 95, 98 (center & right), 101,
    108-109, 111, 112 (all), 113 (all), Back Cover

McNeil, Dan, Denver Center Theatre Company, 63 (left)

Rio Grande Denver-Winter Park Ski Train, 100 (bottom)

Ruhoff, Ron, The Broadmoor, 74 (top left)

Simpich Character Dolls, 56, 59, 112 (bottom), 115

Sizelove, Linda, Redstone Inn, 75 (middle)

United States Air Force Academy, 63 (top left)

Recipe and Menu Index

YES! I wish to support the Colorado Children's Chorale* by ordering additional copies of A COLORADO KIND OF CHRISTMAS.

Please send me:

_____ hardcover copies at $35

_____ softcover copies at $25

ALSO AVAILABLE:
Colorado Children's Chorale audio selections! All proceeds benefit the Chorale.

_____ cassette tape at $9.99

_____ CD at $15.99

❏ Check/Money Order Enclosed (payable to Westcliffe Publishers)

NAME

DAYTIME PHONE NUMBER

STREET ADDRESS

CITY   STATE   ZIP

Bill my   ❏ VISA   ❏ MC

CARD NUMBER   EXP. DATE

SIGNATURE

Books available September 15, 1993; Colorado residents please add 7.3% sales tax. Shipping/handling charges: first item $3.50; each add'l item $1.00.

* A portion of book sales ordered with this form benefits the Colorado Children's Chorale.

WESTCLIFFE PUBLISHERS, P.O. Box 1261, Englewood, CO 80150
Phone 303-935-0900; outside Colorado 800-523-3692; Fax 303-935-0903

YES! I wish to support the Colorado Children's Chorale* by ordering additional copies of A COLORADO KIND OF CHRISTMAS.

Please send me:

_____ hardcover copies at $35

_____ softcover copies at $25

ALSO AVAILABLE:
Colorado Children's Chorale audio selections! All proceeds benefit the Chorale.

_____ cassette tape at $9.99

_____ CD at $15.99

❏ Check/Money Order Enclosed (payable to Westcliffe Publishers)

NAME

DAYTIME PHONE NUMBER

STREET ADDRESS

CITY   STATE   ZIP

Bill my   ❏ VISA   ❏ MC

CARD NUMBER   EXP. DATE

SIGNATURE

Books available September 15, 1993; Colorado residents please add 7.3% sales tax. Shipping/handling charges: first item $3.50; each add'l item $1.00.

* A portion of book sales ordered with this form benefits the Colorado Children's Chorale.

WESTCLIFFE PUBLISHERS, P.O. Box 1261, Englewood, CO 80150
Phone 303-935-0900; outside Colorado 800-523-3692; Fax 303-935-0903

YES! I wish to support the Colorado Children's Chorale* by ordering additional copies of A COLORADO KIND OF CHRISTMAS.

Please send me:

_____ hardcover copies at $35

_____ softcover copies at $25

ALSO AVAILABLE:
Colorado Children's Chorale audio selections! All proceeds benefit the Chorale.

_____ cassette tape at $9.99

_____ CD at $15.99

❏ Check/Money Order Enclosed (payable to Westcliffe Publishers)

NAME

DAYTIME PHONE NUMBER

STREET ADDRESS

CITY   STATE   ZIP

Bill my   ❏ VISA   ❏ MC

CARD NUMBER   EXP. DATE

SIGNATURE

Books available September 15, 1993; Colorado residents please add 7.3% sales tax. Shipping/handling charges: first item $3.50; each add'l item $1.00.

* A portion of book sales ordered with this form benefits the Colorado Children's Chorale.

WESTCLIFFE PUBLISHERS, P.O. Box 1261, Englewood, CO 80150
Phone 303-935-0900; outside Colorado 800-523-3692; Fax 303-935-0903

Return Address

PLACE
STAMP
HERE

Westcliffe Publishers
Post Office Box 1261
Englewood, CO 80150-1261

Return Address

PLACE
STAMP
HERE

Westcliffe Publishers
Post Office Box 1261
Englewood, CO 80150-1261

Return Address

PLACE
STAMP
HERE

Westcliffe Publishers
Post Office Box 1261
Englewood, CO 80150-1261